GW00498886

THE
ROYAL NAVY & THE
PERUVIAN-CHILEAN WAR
1879-1881

To Bebe

The
ROYAL NAVY & THE PERUVIAN-CHILEAN WAR 1879-1881

Rudolph de Lisle's Diaries & Watercolours

Edited by

GERARD DE LISLE F.S.A.

Pen & Sword
MARITIME

First published in Great Britain in 2008 by
PEN & SWORD MARITIME
an imprint of
Pen & Sword Books Limited
47 Church Street, Barnsley
S. Yorkshire, S70 2AS

Copyright © Gerard de Lisle, 2008

ISBN 978 1 84415 652 8

A CIP catalogue record for this book
is available from the British Library.

Typeset in Times New Roman by
Pen & Sword Books Ltd

Printed and bound in Thailand
by Kyodo Nation Printing Services Co., Ltd

Pen & Sword Books Ltd incorporates the imprints of
Pen & Sword Aviation, Pen & Sword Maritime,
Pen & Sword Military,Wharncliffe Local History, Pen & Sword Select,
Pen & Sword Military Classics and Leo Cooper.

For a complete list of Pen & Sword titles please contact:
PEN & SWORD BOOKS LIMITED
47 Church Street, Barnsley, South Yorkshire, S70 2AS, England.
E-mail: enquiries@pen-and-sword.co.uk
Website: www.pen-and-sword.co.uk

Contents

Acknowledgements

After many years of gestation, I am delighted that the diary and watercolours of Lt Rudolph de Lisle RN (1853-1885) will now be published and available for a wider public to enjoy and learn of this unknown War. This could not have been accomplished without the help of my late cousin Everard de Lisle (1930-2003) and his wife Mary Rose, who continues to find me extra data in their archives; Brigadier Henry Wilson, Publishing Manager; Sylvia Menzies-Earl, book designer, and the staff of Pen & Sword Books.

On the Peruvian side, I must thank my wife for her patience whilst I have gleaned odd bits of information in strange corners of the globe; the late Eduardo Orrego (1933-1994), Mayor of Lima 1980–1983, and, last but not least, Dr Celia Wu-Brading who, with her husband Professor David Brading, has written a masterly perspective of this local war, refereed by the main Western powers.

Thanks are also due to numerous friends, acquaintances and institutions:

The Archivist, Admiralty, Whitehall; M.J. Modrell, American Embassy, London; H.A. Vadnais Jr, American Navy Dept, Washington; G. Fitton, Director, Antony Gibbs Holdings Ltd; Mrs D.M. Moss, Librarian and Sarah Hann, Enquiries, BBC Publications; Colin Steele, Bodleian Library (Printed Books); Pablo Butcher, Book Dealer, Dorchester & Miami; Col D.H. B-H-Blundell, British Army Training Team, Sudan; Mr Murphy, British Cemetery, Lima; Military Attache, British Embassy, Khartoum; Commander F. Bromilow RN and Captain F. Hefford RN, British Embassy, Lima; H.E. Roy Maclaren, Canadian Ambassador, London; George Green, Canning House; Fr Patrick McDermott, Catholic Priest, Sheerness, Kent; H.E. Jose Miguel Barras, Chilean Ambassador, Lima; Antonio Figari, Club Nacional, Lima; Paul Goyburu, Collector, Lima; M.M. Grimsley, Colophon Ltd, Leicester; Sr Carlos Milla B, Editorial Milla Batres; G. Greaves (Records), Foreign & Commonwealth Office; M. Esser, German Embassy, London; Herr German Foto-Druppel, Wilhelmshaven; Kurt Reimers, German Maritime Museum, Laboe; A.R.H. Cooper, mss, Guildhall Library, London; Mrs Liz Moore, *Illustrated London News*; Bernard Naylor and Harold Blakemore, Institute of Latin American Studies, University of London; Capt Alfredo Civetta, Italian Embassy, London; Bernard Elliott (1914-1995), Leicestershire Historian; Commander R.D. Wall, Maritime Trust, London; Eduardo Orrego V (1933-1994), Mayor of Lima 1980-1983; Le Conservateur, Musee de la Marine, France; David V. Proctor and C.J. Ware, National Maritime Museum; Admiral Pierre O'Neill, Paris; The Keeper, Public Record Office; H.E. Gilbert Chauny de Porturas-Hoyle, Peruvian Ambassador, London; Jose-Alberto Tejada L, Peruvian Banker; Dr Felix Denegri, Peruvian Historian; Alberto Rubio W, Peruvian Naval Commander (retired); Mariana Rubio, Peru; Cecilia Roeder, Peru; Chantal Langley Cookson, Sotheby's; Jorge Rivera Schreiber.

Naturally, any errors are my responsibility. I would welcome comments of any kind and especially any further information to fill the gaps left blank, or to explain the paucity of data for some of the entries and footnotes.

Introduction by the Editor

Lieutenant Rudolph Edward March Phillipps de Lisle was born on 23 November 1853 at Grace Dieu Manor (built 1835), Leicestershire, an estate which had belonged to the Family since 1692.

He first had tutors but, at the age of 12, he entered Oscott College, near Birmingham. He continued his studies at the Naval Academy, Gosport, and then on the training ship *Britannia* at Dartmouth. He was commissioned as a Naval Officer on 14 March 1873.

Being in the Queen's Navy, he naturally sailed a lot on the high seas, and first came to Peru in HMS *Cameleon*, in November 1871. He returned to South America on HMS *Shannon* in December 1879 and witnessed the Peruvian-Chilean War, recording his experiences in the diaries published here. He left on the same ship in March 1881.

In 1884, General Gordon (1833-1885), who was then Governor of the Sudan, was threatened in Khartoum by fanatical Moslems and this stirred the Christian world. The British Government belatedly sent a rescue expedition with some special Canadian boats and boatmen hopefully capable of passing the Cataracts of the Nile. Unfortunately, it was discovered that these were very different to the rapids of the St Lawrence River and they encountered many problems. On 9 January 1885, it was decided to send a detachment led by Admiral Lord Charles Beresford (1846-1919), which Rudolph joined, across the desert to gain time for Gordon.

This contingent was attacked on 17 January and Rudolph died; Admiral Beresford states, 'De Lisle had his whole face cut clean off' at the battle of Abu Klea, north-east of Khartoum. He was buried on the battlefield and the graves and memorial are still extant. The survivors continued towards the Capital but, on arriving nearby on 28 January, they were informed that General Gordon had been captured and assassinated on 26 January.

In the middle of the last century, people did not have the amusements of today and so they entertained themselves with music, painting and the arts in general. Rudolph, like the rest of his family, was no mean draughtsman and this proved useful in the Navy. He drew maps and pictures of the different places and events which he saw. He even had a few sketches published in the *Illustrated London News*.

Unfortunately, the majority of his letters (written regularly to his parents) no longer exist except as published in his Biography. His life, though short, was very interesting and there are three editions of this work. In a few letters he mentions his drawings and the places visited. For example, he writes from HMS *Shannon* at Callao 8 June 1880, 'Made several sketches prior to a preliminary climb in anticipation of Mt Meiggs' (17000 feet). The author of this biography, Rev H N Oxenham (1829-1888) states in his *Memoir of Lt Rudolph de Lisle RN*:

> 'The *Shannon* soon afterwards sailed for South America, being ordered to the coast of Chile and Peru during the war between the two States, and reached Callao in December, which continued to be their ordinary station for more than a twelvemonth, though they touched at Iquique, Chimbote, and other points on the Chilean and Peruvian coasts. Rudolph was now in a region familiar to him ten years before, when on the *Cameleon*, and he found many old friends at Lima and elsewhere, and had a great deal of amusement in the way of dancing and private theatricals, as well as cricket and shooting, the latter, however, not being so good as in Beshika Bay; he also got through a fair amount of drawing.' (p.96/7)

Many of the watercolours have probably disappeared but luckily many surfaced rather suddenly in 1967 from Saskatchewan, Canada. His youngest brother (of 16 children), Gerard, had taken them there in 1905.

When I began to look after the family archives, I found that there were private effects of Gerard (1860-1924) in Canada which had not been collected since he died there. In 1968 these belongings were sent to me and, to my surprise and delight, discovered that many watercolours were by Rudolph, and referred to the war between Peru and Chile (1879-1883).

My wife, being Anglo-Peruvian, and I were thrilled to receive these historic, artistic, unique and impartial watercolours.

On 12 August 1970, due to the interest of Senor Eduardo Orrego (Mayor of Lima 1980-1983) and the Peruvian Ambassador in London, I presented coloured copies of thirty-six watercolours to the Prime Minister and Minister of War of Peru. I was accompanied by our son Freddie and the British Ambassador (Sir) Hugh Morgan. The Prime Minister thanked us and informed us that he would lodge them in the Centre for Historical-Military studies in Lima. As a result of this presentation, illustrated articles were published in different Lima newspapers and periodicals including *La Prensa, El Comercio* and *Oiga*.

During that trip to Lima, I happened to pass a bookshop in the Miraflores district and noticed a book in the window entitled, *Guerra con Chile...Campana del Sur... Abril-Diciembre 1879*, by the Peruvian historian Fr Ruben Vargas Ugarte SJ (1886-1975). I therefore bought it and

wrote to him also asking to purchase Volume 2: *La Campana de Tacna y de Lima 1880-1881.*
Afterwards, I found the following:

1. *Six weeks with the Chilean Army being a short account of a march from Pisco to Lurin and of the attack on Lima,* by William Acland (1847-1924), Commander Royal Navy 1880. Published for private circulation. Printed at the Melanesian Mission, Norfolk Island (Pacific Ocean).
2. *Sketches of War 1879-1880*, by R B Boyd, 1881.
3. *War between Peru & Chile 1879-1882*, by (Sir) Clements R Markham (1830-1916), London, 3rd Edition 1883.

Fr Vargas informed me that he was in the middle of producing his Obra Maestra: the *Historia General del Peru* in ten volumes and he requested that some watercolours by Rudolph should be reproduced in Volume X.

Thanks to all these books and other studies of this period, I have been able to complete and increase the captions of Rudolph: some were very short, others did not have dates, but all are of great interest.

In 1979, during another visit to South America, I visited the British Embassy in Lima and the Naval Attache, Captain F Herford RN, showed me the xerox of a Diary by Rudolph de Lisle which he had recently received from the Naval Historical branch of the Ministry of Defence. This had been loaned to them by my cousin, Major Everard de Lisle (1930-2003). We come full circle!

It therefore gives me great pleasure to present this important collection; the seventeen watercolours already published by Fr Vargas, many of the other remaining watercolours and the fascinating Diary which covers a large amount of the time Rudolph spent in Peru and cruising the west coast of South America.

I am sure that this work will be of historical value not only to Peruvians, Bolivians and Chileans, but also to academics and amateur historians throughout the world.

I hope that the reader will enjoy this record as much as I have while compiling and editing it.

Gerard de Lisle
August 2008

Lieutenant Rudolph M.P. de Lisle R.N.

Lieutenant Rudolph M.P. de Lisle, R.N.
(1853-1885)

Surname:		March Phillipps de Lisle	
Names:		Rudolph Edward	
Birth:		23 November 1853	
Place:		Grace Dieu Manor, Leicestershire, England	
Education:		Oscott College, Nr. Birmingham	Sept 1865 – June 1866
		Naval Academy, Gosport, Hants.	Oct 1866 – Apr 1867
		Britannia, Dartmouth	May 1867 – July 1868
Service:	i	HMS *Victory*	July 1868 – Sept 1868
	ii	HMS *Bristol* etc.	Sept 1868 – Apr 1869
		(Gibraltar, Malta, Syracuse, Naples)	
	iii	The Flying Squadron (Rio, Vancouver, Honolulu,	June 1869 – Dec 1870
		Australia & New Zealand, Valparaiso, Bahia (Brazil))	
	iv	HMS *Cameleon* etc.	Apr 1871 – May 1875
		(Callao, Lima, Tahiti, Valparaiso)	
	v	Naval College, Greenwich	July 1875 – Apr 1876
	vi	Mediterranean Squadron	May 1876 – Oct 1879 (c.)
		(Montenegro, Athens, Smyrna)	
	vii	Pacific Squadron, HMS *Shannon*	Dec 1879 – June 1881
		(Chilean–Peruvian War)	
	viii	Naval College, Greenwich	Oct 1881 – July 1882
	ix	Mediterranean (Malta, Venice, Cyprus)	Jan 1883 – June 1884
	x	Egypt – Sudan, HMS *Alexandra*	June 1884 – Jan 1885

Death:	17 January 1885
Place:	Abu Klea Battle, Sudan
Burial:	17 January 1885
Place:	Abu Klea Battlefield, Sudan
Decorations:	Egyptian Campaign Medal (Q.Victoria)
	With 2 clasps: 'Abu Klea' 'The Nile 1884-85'
Commemorations:	Sheerness (R.C.) Church, Kent: Pulpit with de Lisle Coat of Arms and Plaque
	inscribed 'to the Catholics who fell when serving in Naval Brigade'
Memoirs:	*Memoir of Lt. Rudolph de Lisle RN* by Rev. H.N. Oxenham, M.A. London
	1st Edition, March 1886, 2nd Edition, September 1886, 3rd Edition, 1887

Introduccion del Editor

A l Teniente de la Marina Inglesa, Rudolph Edward March Phillipps de Lisle, nacío el 23 de noviembre de 1853 en el Castillo de Grace- dieu Manor – perteneciente a la familia desde 1692 – en el Condado de Leicestershire, Inglaterra.

Sus primeros estudios los realizó bajo la dirección de tutores y a los 12 años ingresó al Colegio de Oscott, cerca de Birmingham. Continuó sus estudios en la Academia Naval, Gosport, y a bordo del Buque-escuela *Britannia* en Dartmouth. Se graduó Oficial de la Marina de Guerra Britanica el 14 marzo de 1873.

Rudolph navegó por diferentes partes del mundo y llegó al Perú por primera vez, en el buque *Cameleon*, en noviembre de 1871; regresó por segunda vez, en el buque *Shannon*, en diciembre de 1879 y, despues de permanecer mas de un año en ésas costas, partió en el mismo buque en marzo de 1881.

En 1884, el General Gordon, que en ésa epoca era Gobernador del Sudan, fué asaltado en Khartoum por fanaticos musulmanes y eso conmovió mucho al mundo Cristiano. El Gobierno Británico envió una expedición de rescate con buques & barqueros canadienses especiales para poder pasar las Cataratas del Nilo; desgraciadamente encontraron que éstas eran muy diferentes a los Rapids del Rio St Lawrence y tuvieron muchas dificultades. El 9 de enero de 1885 un destacamento (entre los cuales se encontraba Rudolph) bajó a tierra para seguir el camino a pie y ganar tiempo cruzando parte del desierto.

El destacamento fue asaltado el 17 de enero de 1885 por dervishes y Rudolph murió por lanzas musulmanas en la Batalla de Abu-Klea al nor-este de Khartoum; fué enterrado en el campo de batalla. Los sobrevivientes siguieron adelante, pero cuando se acercaron a la Capital el 28 de enero, recibieron la noticia que el General Gordon había sido capturado y asesinado el 26 de enero.

A mediados del siglo pasado, al no existir las distracciones de nuestra época, la sociedad se entretenia tocando instrumentos de música, pintando y practicando los artes en general. A Rudolph, como al resto de su familia, le agradaba el dibujo y poséia especiales dotes en este arte. Lo cual fue una ventaja al entrar en la Marina pues le fue muy útil para hacer mapas y dibujos de los diferentes sitios y acontecimientos de interes que presenciaba, los que solía enviar a Inglaterra y algunos de ellos fueron publicados en el *Illustrated London News*!

Desgraciadamente la mayoría de las cartas, que escribia regularmente a sus padres, ya no existen, peru su biografía – su vida aunque corta fué muy interesante – se publicó en tres ediciones en 1886-1887. Varias de sus cartas fueron reproducidas en ésta obra y en algunas, habla de sus dibujo y de los sitios visitados. Por ejemplo escribió desde HMS *Shannon* en el Callao el 8 de Junio de 1880: '…..Hice algunos dibujos antes de hacer una subida preliminaria en anticipación (de subir) al Monte Meiggs….'

El autor de esta biografia, el Rev H M Oxenham, dice

> 'El *Shannon*…navegó por Sur America, enviado a las costas de Chile y Peru durante la Guerra entre los dos países y llegó al Callao en diciembre (1879) donde su buque ancló por más de doce meses aunque navegó ocasionalmente a Iquique, Chimbote y otros puntos de las costa chilena y peruana…Rudolph produjo un buen número de dibujos.'

Muchas de sus acuarelas han desaparacido – pero con suerte algunas aparecieron de nuevo en 1967 en Saskatchewan (Canada); Gerard, el hermano menor, los habia llevado al Canada en 1905. Cuando yo commencé a ocuparme de los archivos familiares encontré que todavía existían efectos personales que no habían sido reclamados por la familia después de su muerte en 1924. En 1968, me fueron enviados y tuve la sorpresa encontrar que muchas acuarelas eran de Rudolph y se referian al conflicto chileno-peruano.

Siendo mi esposa anglo-peruana nos interesaron mucho tanto artísticamente como por su gran valor historico.

El 12 de agosto de 1970, por intermedio del Arquitecto Eduardo Orrego (1933-1994) y del Embajador peruano en Londres, presente las copias de 36 acuarelas en colores al Premier y Ministro de Guerra del Perú. Hice las presentaciones acompanado por el Embajador Britanico (Sir) Hugh Morgan y nuestro hijo Freddie. El Premier nos informó que las entregaría al Centro de Estudios Historico-Militares; con ése motivo, articulos ilustrados fueron publicados por La Prensa, El Comercio, otros periodicos y la revista Oiga de Lima.

En la occasion de mi visita a Lima, al pasar frente a una libreria en Miraflores, encontre que exhibian el libro *Guerra con Chile, Campaña del Sur,* abril-diciembre 1879 por el historiador peruano Padre Ruben Vargas Ugarte SJ. Lo compré y le escribí para pedirle el Segundo volumen

La Campaña de Tacna y de Lima 1880-1881. Despues encontré los siguientes libros además de los mencionados anteriormente:

1. *Six weeks with the Chilean Army being a short account of a march from Pisco to Lurin and of the attack on Lima* by William Acland (1847-1924), Commander Royal Navy 1880. Impresa para circulación privada en la imprenta de la Mision de Melanesia (Norfolk Island) en el Oceano Pacífico.
2. *Sketches of War 1879-1880*, by R B Boyd, 1881
3. *War between Peru & Chile 1879-1882*, by (Sir) Clements R Markham (1830-1916) London, 3rd Edition, 1883.

Al ponerme en contacto con el Padre Vargas (1886-1975), encontre que estaba en plena producción de su obra maestra en diez volumenes *Historia General del Peru* editado por el Señor Carlos Milla Batres, y decidimos incluir varias acuarelas de Rudolph.

Gracias a todas éstas obras y a otros estudios míos de ésa epoca, he podido completar los diversos acontecimientos, captados por el arte de Rudolph, en acuarelas y dibujos; algunos son pequeños, otros no tienen fechas pero todos son de gran interés.

Ahora tengo el placer de presentar esta valiosa colección, las 17 acuarelas ya incorporadas en el volumen 10 de la *Historia General del Perú* así como el resto de las colleccíon referente a Sur America. El señor Milla, con su gran labor en editar éste libro, ha encontrado una manera muy apropiada e imparcial de commemorar el primer centenario de la Guerra con Chile.

Estoy seguro que éstas 59 acuarelas serán de valor histórico tanto para peruanos, bolivianos y chilenos como para profesores y aficionados mundiales de la historia marítima.

Espero que los lectores de ésta obra disfruten su contenido con el mismo placer que experimenté al escribir éstas lineas de introduccion.

Gerard de Lisle
August 2008

Lieutenant Rudolph M.P. de Lisle, R.N.
(1853-1885)

Apellido:	March Phillipps de Lisle	
Nombres:	Rudolph Edward	
Nacimiento:	23 November 1853	
Sitio:	Grace Dieu Manor, Leicestershire, England	

Educacion:	Colegio Oscott, Cerca de Birmingham	Sept 1865 – June 1866
	Academia Naval, Gosport, Hants.	Oct 1866 – Apr 1867
	Britannia, Dartmouth	May 1867 – July 1868

Servicio Militar:	i	HMS *Victory*	July 1868 – Sept 1868
	ii	HMS *Bristol* etc.	Sept 1868 – Apr 1869
		(Gibraltar, Malta, Syracuse, Naples)	
	iii	La Flota Volante (Rio, Vancouver, Honolulu,	June 1869 – Dec 1870
		Australia & New Zealand, Valparaiso, Bahia (Brazil))	
	iv	HMS *Cameleon* etc.	Apr 1871 – May 1875
		(Callao, Lima, Tahiti, Valparaiso)	
	v	Colegio Naval, Greenwich	July 1875 – Apr 1876
	vi	La Flota del Mediterraneo	May 1876 – Oct 1879 (c.)
		(Montenegro, Athens, Smyrna)	
	vii	La Flota del Pacifico, HMS *Shannon*	Dec 1879 – June 1881
		(Guerra entre Chile y Peru)	
	viii	Colegio Naval, Greenwich	Oct 1881 – July 1882
	ix	Mediterraneo (Malta, Venice, Cyprus)	Jan 1883 – June 1884
	x	Egipto – Sudan, HMS Alexandra	June 1884 – Jan 1885

Muerte:	17 Enero, 1885
Sitio:	Batalla de Abu Klea, Sudan
Entierro:	17 Enero, 1885
Sitio:	Campo de Batalla, Abu Klea, Sudan

Condecoraciones:	Medalla Campana de Egipto (Reina Victoria)
	Con 2 broches: 'Abu Klea' y 'The Nile 1884-85'

Commemoraciones:	Iglesia Catolica de Sheerness, Kent, Inglaterra: Pulpito con Escudo Armorial de la familia de Lisle y Plaqua commemorando los Catolicos que fallecieron con la Brigada Naval

Memoirs:	*Memoir of Lt. Rudolph de Lisle RN* by Rev. H.N. Oxenham, M.A. London 1st Edition, March 1886, 2nd Edition, September 1886, 3rd Edition, 1887

THE WAR OF THE PACIFIC:

A British Naval Perspective

by

Dr Celia Wu-Brading

The War

In the War of the Pacific, 1879-1883, Chile fought a series of battles at sea and on land against Bolivia and Peru, which culminated in the occupation of Lima. Victory rewarded Chile with the permanent cession of the Bolivian province of Atacama and the Peruvian province of Tarapacá and port of Arica, provinces endowed with great mineral wealth. If the war attracted international attention, it was because South America, hitherto the scene of civil strife, had by then entered upon a cycle of economic growth based upon the export of mineral and agricultural produce and, in the case of Peru, of guano. Foreign investors and entrepreneurs, mainly British, had financed the construction of railways and port facilities. The flow of capital and business expertise was matched by extensive European immigration, most numerous in Argentina and Brazil, but present in most countries in the southern hemisphere. The 1876 census of Lima, for example, enumerated 100,156 inhabitants, of whom 17,922 were foreign-born, among whom 6,518 came from Europe and North America, 5,624 from China, and the rest from adjacent republics.[1] In their ranks were to be found merchants, shopkeepers, artisans and mechanics. Immigration and foreign investment were assisted by the improvement in telegraphic communication and transport by steamships. The British owned Pacific Steam Navigation Company, which had its headquarters at Valparaíso, despatched steamers up and down the Pacific coast. The interests of the immigrant communities were safeguarded by the presence of the diplomatic ministers of the leading maritime powers, representatives who, if needed, could call upon the material power of the

---

1   For a discussion of this census see *Testimonios británicos de la ocupación chilena de Lima*, ed. Celia Wu-Brading, 'Introducción', pp.7-8.

navies of Great Britain, France, the United States, Italy and Germany, which all despatched warships to patrol the coasts of the Pacific ocean. When war was declared in 1879 between Chile and its northern neighbours, European and American diplomats and naval commanders immediately sought assurances that the lives and property of their citizens would be respected.

The cause of the conflict was a long-standing dispute between Chile and Bolivia as to whether the boundary of the Atacama province should be drawn along the 23rd parallel of latitude, as Chile claimed, or along the 25th parallel, as Bolivia claimed. In the treaties of 1866 and 1874, a compromise frontier was fixed at the 24th parallel and both countries agreed to exploit the newly discovered mineral wealth of the zone without increase in taxation. The main company which invested in the extraction of silver and nitrates, however, was Chilean, albeit backed by British investors, and relied on an imported Chilean labour force. When the government of Bolivia imposed a new ten percent tax on the produce of all mines in the Atacama province without consultation, and swiftly embargoed these properties when managers refused to pay the tax, on 14 February 1879, a small Chilean force seized possession of the port of Antofagasta, and proclaimed Chilean sovereignty over all territory below the 23rd parallel. These dramatic events prompted President Mariano Ignacio Prado of Peru to despatch a diplomatic mission to Santiago de Chile to mediate, especially since the governments of Peru and Bolivia had signed a treaty in 1873 which guaranteed the territorial integrity of both republics and established a mutual defence pact against foreign aggression. Following the failure of this initiative, on 5 April 1879, Chile formally declared war on Bolivia and Peru.[2]

The first phase of the war was fought at sea, since the barren, deserted landscape of Tarapacá, Peru's southern most coastal province, prohibited any invasion by land. But to invade by sea required numerous transport ships and without maritime supremacy they could easily be sunk or captured by hostile action. If the ensuing engagements at sea commanded international attention, it was because naval technology was still in the midst of a far-reaching revolution. Although the first steamships were employed in the 1820s, they were relatively slow, clumsy, and coast-bound vessels. It was not until 1858, when the French launched *La Gloire*, that the first steam-propelled ironclad warship appeared on the seas and thereby rendered obsolescent almost three hundred years of naval architecture and strategy. In the twenty years that followed,

---

2   For the origins of the war see William F. Sater, *Chile and the War of the Pacific* (Lincoln, Nebraska, 1986), pp.5-19; see also Jorge Basadre, *Historia de la República del Perú 1822-1933, sexta edición aumentada y corregida* 16 Vols. (Lima, 1969) VIII, 7-64.

a confusing array of warships were constructed by the world's maritime powers, in which there can be discerned a dialectical process, in which, as ships became larger and their guns fewer and more powerful, so equally the protective iron armouring of these vessels became ever more thick. At first, ramming of enemy ships was promoted as an essential tactic, only to be discarded as naval artillery acquired ever greater range.[3] All these developments took time to implement and, during the War of the Pacific, many warships made of wood were still in action. Moreover, the prodigious amounts of coal consumed by battleships obliged naval architects to provide the vessels that patrolled distant oceans with a three mast rig of sails. It was to take the British navy more than a generation to establish a worldwide system of coaling stations and thereby eliminate any further reliance on sail.

The rapid development of naval technology also allowed minor maritime powers to purchase warships, recently built in Europe, which could challenge vessels of the leading powers that had been constructed at an earlier date. An example of this possibility occurred in May 1877 when Nicolás de Piérola, a dissident Peruvian politician, seized the turret ship *Huáscar* at Callao harbour and then steamed up and down the coast, bombarding towns. Since the Peruvian government refused to act, Rear Admiral de Horsey, the commander of the British Pacific squadron, decided to compel her surrender, only to find that he did not possess any obvious superiority over his opponent. The *Huáscar* had been built by Lairds at Birkenhead in 1865, and was a 1,130 ton, single turret ship carrying two 10-inch Armstrong guns throwing a 300-lb projectile. Her turret armour was five inches and the side armour four inches in thickness. Her speed was only ten knots. Admiral de Horsey's flagship was the *Shah*, an unarmoured frigate which carried two 9 inch, 12 ton guns and eight 7 inch guns on each side. He also had in support, the corvette *Amethyst* of 1,970 tons armed with fourteen 65 pound guns. In the event, the *Shah*'s guns proved ineffectual against the *Huáscar*'s armour and the ship was obliged to engage in constant manoeuvres to avoid being rammed or hit by the *Huáscar*'s shells. The engagement ended when Piérola entered harbour and surrendered to the Peruvian navy.[4]

Two years later, in May 1879, the *Huáscar*, by then the flagship of Admiral Miguel Grau, led the attack on the Chilean fleet. It was supported by the frigate *Independencia*, built on the Thames in 1865, of 2,004 tons, with 4½ inch armour and one gun of 250 pound shells and another of 150. Apart from these two antiquated ironclads, Peru only possessed two wooden corvettes, the *Unión* of 1,150 tons and the *Pilcomayo* of 600 tons. In addition, two 'monitors', with 10 inch armour

---

3   On the introduction of ironclads see Peter Padfield, *The Battleship Era* (London, 1972), passim.
4   *Ibid.*, pp.94-5.

on their turrets, had been purchased in 1869 from the United States and renamed as *Atahualpa* and *Manco Cápac*. Each had two 15 inch Rodman guns, but their engines could not achieve more than 4 knots, so that they were used as floating batteries, stationed permanently in the harbours of Callao and Arica. With the onset of war, the Chileans found that their ironclads required refitting and patrolled the coast with their lesser warships. On 21 May 1879 the *Huáscar* and *Independencia* approached the harbour of Iquique, the principal port of the province of Tarapacá, where they encountered two Chilean warships, the *Esmeralda*, a wooden corvette of 850 tons armed with 12 forty pound guns, and the *Covadonga*, a wooden gunboat of 600 tons with two 70 pounders. What followed is described by the manager of the Tarapacá Nitrate Company, printed in Appendix I. The *Huáscar* relied on its armour for protection from enemy artillery and simply moved swiftly to ram the *Esmeralda* twice over. On the second occasion, the Chilean commander, Captain Arturo Prat 'leaped on board the *Huáscar*, revolver in hand, followed by a daring few, but they were down almost before they had time to strike a blow. Captain Prat got as far as the turret where he killed Lieutenant S. Velarde but was himself shot the moment after by a seaman'. By then, although the *Esmeralda* was sinking, the *Huáscar* rammed her for a third time, and she sank with the loss of most of her crew.[5]

The Peruvian victory, however, was soon overcome by disaster, since the *Covadonga* had fled south, pursued by the *Independencia*. Taking advantage of its small size and knowledge of the coast, the Chilean vessel manoeuvred skilfully and succeeded in enticing its pursuer to follow inshore, with the result that the *Independencia* 'crashed with all her weight and the force of her powerful engines onto the rocks'. Although the *Huáscar* sought to tow her off, the ship could not be moved and had to be abandoned, her crew taken on board the flagship. In the months that followed, Admiral Grau, assisted by the wooden corvette *Unión* dominated the sea and raided the coasts and port of Antofagasta. He also captured a Chilean troopship, *Rimac*, which had on board a regiment of cavalry. In this initial phase of the war, Grau and the *Huáscar*, as the Peruvian historian, Jorge Basadre wrote, were 'the only sword and the only shield of Peru that detained the invasion during six long months'.[6]

However, once the Chilean fleet had been refitted, its strength proved overwhelming, especially after the loss of the *Independencia*, since they possessed twin ironclads, *Almirante Cochrane* and *Blanco Encalada*, each of 3,560 tons, constructed at Hull in 1875, protected by

---

5   For the relative strengths of the Peruvian and Chilian navies, see Clements R. Markham, *The War between Peru and Chile, 1879-1882* (London, 1882), pp.93-6. See also Appendix I, letter of the Manager of the Tarapacá Nitrate Company, 27 May 1879.
6   On Grau see Basadre, *Historia de la República*, VIII, pp.88-107; the quotation occurs on p.101.

9 inch armour and equipped with six 12 ton Armstrong guns with 250 pound shells. In addition, Chile had two iron corvettes, *Chacabuco* and the *O'Higgins*, armed with three 7 ton Armstrong guns. It was on 8 October 1879 that off Point Angamos, the *Huáscar* and *Unión* were cornered in the Bay of Mejillones by the two Chilean ironclads. Their superior firepower was such that Grau and his officers were all killed when the command post in the flagship's turret was destroyed. So demoralised were the crew that the Chileans were able to board the vessel, extinguish the fires, and take it back to Valparaíso for repair. The *Unión* escaped northwards, assisted by its light weight and speed.[7] But from this time on, the Chileans dominated the sea and were free to land their troops wherever they wished.

The Journal

The main purpose of this book is to publish the journal and watercolours of Rudolph de Lisle (1853-1885), a naval lieutenant who arrived in Valparaíso on board HMS *Shannon* in October 1879 and was a witness of the Chilean capture of Lima in January 1881. He was the eighth son and fourteenth child of Ambrose Phillipps de Lisle, a wealthy landowner and an influential Catholic convert, who was the founder of the Cistercian monastery of Mount St Bernard in Charnwood Forest and a patron of the neo-Gothic architect, Augustus Welby Pugin. His mother was Laura Clifford, granddaughter of the fourth Lord Clifford of Chudleigh. An elder brother, Everard Lisle Phillipps, had been awarded a posthumous Victoria Cross for his valiant service in the capture of Delhi during the Indian Mutiny of 1857.[8] Rudolph was educated in the Catholic college of St Mary's Oscott, before entering a naval academy in preparation for a year on the *Britannia* training ship at Dartmouth, from which he graduated as a midshipman in July 1866. In that capacity he promptly embarked on a cruise first across the Mediterranean and then around the world. As one of the rare Catholic officers in the British navy, he was invariably charged with the duty, when in the appropriate harbour, of conducting Catholic ratings to attend mass on Sundays. Although his father had once advocated a grand union of the Catholic, Orthodox and Anglican Churches (a proposal that elicited a swift reprimand from the Vatican),

7   Markham, *The War between Peru and Chile*, pp.93-4, 120-32.
8   Rev. H.N. Oxenham, *Memoir of Lieutenant Rudolph de Lisle R.N. of the Naval Brigade of the Upper Nile* (London, 1886), pp.3-8. For his brother Everard see Edmund Sheridan Purcell, *Life and Letters of Ambrose Phillipps de Lisle*, edited and finished by Edwin de Lisle, 2 vols. (London, 1900), II, 314-16.

Rudolph was not at all impressed by his visits to churches in Greece, since he wrote, 'Their religion is really a kind of fetichism, and what is called by Protestants Mariolatry in our Church, would have to be called *idolatry* pure and simple in theirs'. When he sailed to South America in 1872, he was shocked by the immorality of the Catholic clergy in that region and, on attending mass in local churches, he found that 'a Holy Sacrifice was made into a sacrilege'.[9] In effect, his Catholicism was decidedly Victorian and made little allowance for cultural differences.

It was at the age of 19, still a midshipman on board HMS *Camelon*, that he first visited Lima. He found it to be 'a miserable city', apart from the churches, since he praised the cathedral as 'a splendid building'. Nor did its inhabitants attract him, since he wrote to his mother, 'The Peruvians are chiefly Spaniards mixed with Indians, and there are now no true Incas. They are a miserable set of creatures'. His dismal impression of Peru was in part determined by the atrocious sequence of events set in motion when, in July 1872, Tomás Gutiérrez, the Minister of War in the outgoing government of Colonel José Balta, staged a coup to avert the accession of Manuel Pardo as president. His three brothers proclaimed Tomás to be President, first imprisoned and then murdered Balta, but failed to seize Pardo, who took refuge on board the *Huáscar*, then commanded by Miguel Grau. But Congress and public opinion failed to recognise the coup, military support soon ebbed, and the mob of the capital rioted and killed the Minister and two of his brothers. A wretched climax was achieved when the naked bodies of Tomás and Silvestre Gutiérrez were hung from the towers of the cathedral, only later to be burnt in the main square of Lima. The young de Lisle wrote a garbled, scandalised account of this coup in a letter to his mother.[10]

After his return to England, de Lisle spent a year at the Royal Naval College at Greenwich and graduated as lieutenant. In January 1879 he joined the complement of HMS *Shannon* which, after a cruise in the Mediterranean in July, was ordered to set sail for Peru, there to join HMS *Triumph*, the flagship of Rear Admiral Frederick H. Stirling, the commander of the Pacific Squadron. The *Shannon* was a fully armoured cruiser, launched in 1877, with a weight of 5,560 tons and equipped with two 18 ton guns of 10 inch calibre in its bows and another seven 12 ton guns of 9 inch calibre. It had a detached ram, which was never used. Since its bunker capacity only covered 560 tons of coal, the ship relied on the sails of its three masts to carry it across the oceans. According to a later account, the *Shannon* was remarkably slow, only achieving 12.2

---

9 Oxenham, *Memoir*, pp.46-7, 82, 149.
10 *Ibid.*, pp.48-9, 53. De Lisle called these brothers 'Guitanis'. For an account of this attempted coup see Basadre, *Historia de la República*, VI, 364-73. Journal p.72

knots under steam; moreover, its captain was advised never to practise firing his two heavy guns, since their shells were too heavy and expensive to be sent to the Pacific station. *Triumph* was a battleship, completed in 1873, with a weight of 6,640 tons, and equipped with ten 9 inch calibre guns, and also depended on its sails for oceanic voyages. Taken together, these two warships were more than a match for the Chilean fleet and their presence demonstrated that the Admiralty sought to obliterate the humiliation suffered by the *Shah*.[11]

Here is no place to comment on de Lisle's journal entries about his cruise around the Mediterranean, still less discuss his dutiful description of Rome and its churches. To reach Peru, the *Shannon* sailed via Madeira and Rio de Janeiro before passing through the Magellan Strait to reach Valparaíso on 16 October. There, anchored in the harbour, was the damaged, captured *Huáscar*. De Lisle offered a description of the battle at Point Angamos, close to the port of Antofagasta, and also drew a sketch map of the movements of the ships during the engagement. His comments reveal the close professional interest of a naval officer in the relative firepower and performance of the ships involved in this action. From Valparaíso, the *Shannon* sailed northwards to Coquimbo, where it took in 375 tons of coal and then moved to Antofagasta, when news came that Chilean troopships had sailed on 2 November for the Peruvian port of Arica. He commented that, 'Arica is the first place after leaving Coquimbo where one sees a blade of grass or a tree... For hundreds of miles one passes up the coast seeing nothing but the same desert hills...'. It was at Pisagua that the *Shannon* encountered fifteen Chilean warships and transports, a port from which the Bolivian defence force had been quickly dislodged and where close to 10,000 men were landed. De Lisle was impressed by the equipment of the Chilean soldiers and by their 35 Krupps field-guns. He commented, 'The Chileans have complete command of the sea and can land anywhere they choose. Strange that perhaps the fate of a country should depend upon the loss of a single ship...'. Confined on board the *Shannon* however, de Lisle had no means of following the course of the war on land, where in successive engagements at Dolores and Tarapacá, the Chileans defeated the combined Bolivian and Peruvian forces and thereby gained control of the entire Peruvian province of Tarapacá and its wealthy nitrate mines.[12]

Instead, the *Shannon* moved north to Arica, where it encountered French and American warships. It was there that de Lisle commented on the Peruvian enmity to Great Britain:

---

11 Oxenham, *Memoir,* pp.89-109. For photographs and precise measurements of the *Triumph* and the *Shannon* see Oscar Parkes, *British Battleships. "Warrior" 1860 to "Vanguard" 1950. A History of Design, Construction and Armament,* a new and revised edition (London, 1970), pp.156-59, 234-38.
12 Rudolph de Lisle, *Journal,* entries 16 October to 10 November 1879.

The Peruvians refused to allow us to see any of the works inside, so great is their dislike of us; but it is the same everywhere on the Peruvian coast, and the *Huáscar* and *Shah* affair is the cause; we have not added laurels to the English Naval history by this business, though in the Lists of Meritorious acts etc. in the Navy List everyone who was present in the action is mentioned as though it had been a glorious victory. (Entry Arica *c.*7 December 1879)

On 13 December 1879 he witnessed some 2,000 Peruvian troops entering Arica, raising the number of defenders to about 8,000. He added, 'They do not compare with the Chilean troops in appearance, discipline or equipment and are nearly all full-bloodied Indians…'. The *Shannon* then sailed to Callao, the port of Lima where, apart from the *Triumph*, it encountered the *Victorieuse*, the ironclad flagship of Admiral Abel Bergasse du Petit Thouars, the commander of the French Pacific squadron. It was at Callao that he learnt that President Mariano Ignacio Prado had chosen to leave Peru and that, after considerable public commotion, Nicolás de Piérola became president, of whom he wrote, 'this man seems to be acknowledged as the most capable man, though utterly unscrupulous and as big a robber as any'. He added, 'Since the loss of the *Huáscar* the nation has gone into mourning; no parties or gaiety of any sort, no dances, for the populace would break anyone's windows who permitted it'. After a description of what remained of the Peruvian fleet, he noted that the crew of the *Shannon* had competed in sailing races with the *Triumph* and they also played games of baseball and cricket with the crew of the American warship, US *Pansacola*, adding, 'we were all very sorry when she left, for she had a very nice lot of fellows on board and the two ships were very friendly'. He also attended midnight mass on Christmas Eve at the church of La Merced, which he found to be 'well done', if ill-attended.[13]

On learning that the Chilean navy had bombarded the port of Arica on 8 March 1880, the *Shannon* weighed anchor and moved southwards, and soon found that some 16,000 Chilean soldiers had landed at the port of Ylo. De Lisle was impressed by the *Angamos*, a ship recently purchased by Chile, which for six consecutive days fired from 12 to 15 shots a day into Arica from a range of 8,000 yards. The ship had but one powerful gun, 'an improved Armstrong', 111 tons in weight, 8 inch in calibre, with shells of 180 lbs and a barrel length of 18 foot 4 inches, a length which, together with a greater intake of gunpowder, accounted for its 8,000 yards range.[14] He also provided a complete description of the surprise entrance of the *Unión*, the Peruvian corvette, into the harbour of Arica and its equally daring escape. At the end of March the *Shannon* returned to Callao, where the Chilean ironclads had assembled, determined to

---

13 *Ibid.*, entries 7 December 1879 to 21 January 1880
14 *Ibid.*, entry 29 February 1880.

attack the Peruvian warships that were protected by the port's extensive fortifications. By this time an array of neutral warships, French, Italian, German and American, were stationed in the bay, summoned to protect their citizens who resided in Lima. De Lisle noted that the Pacific Steam Navigation Company's ships had abandoned Callao in favour of the port of Chimbote. In negotiations with the Chileans designed to ensure that neutral merchant shipping was not caught up in the blockade, the French Rear Admiral Petit Thouars took the lead. In the ensuing bombardment of Callao, the Chileans mortified the Peruvians by employing the *Huáscar*, which had been refitted for battle. But their fleet was careful to remain beyond the range of the Peruvian guns and of the torpedoes that were kept ready in the harbour. As the bombardment continued, the neutral warships often developed warm social relations. Thus, de Lisle recorded that he attended a farewell reception aboard a German warship, adding,

> The *Hansa* and ourselves were great friends and a hardworking lot they were; there is no doubt the Germans are thoroughly in earnest and intend to make their officers and men (if possible) decidedly efficient, it is amusing to hear the Frenchmen ask whether we considered they (Germans) were improving. The officers of these two nations have no intercourse, the Captains alone doing the formal and necessary calls.

Obviously, the memory of the 1870 war was still all too close.[15]

Throughout his journal, de Lisle provided a detailed analysis of the Chilean bombardment and the performance of the various ships and their guns, annotations based on his own expertise as a naval officer. But he also took time to draw a large number of watercolour or pencil sketches of ships, harbours and bays, all done with a professional skill, and which add immensely to the value of his observations.

It was at the beginning of June 1880 that he accompanied a group of officers and men from the *Shannon* to take the famous railway from Lima to La Oroya, which by then reached to the small town of Chicla situated at 12,220 ft amidst the Andean highlands. He and a companion then climbed up to the summit of Mount Meiggs, another 2,000 ft, an exploit that gave him a splitting headache. In a letter to his mother, he commented that at the hotel in Chicla the group celebrated the anniversary of 'the *Shannon* and *Chesapeake* action' with hot punch, speeches and songs, 'having ascertained there were no Yankees in the hotel'. He also took care to draw some striking sketches of the Andean landscape.[16]

15 *Ibid.*, entry 25 May 1880
16 *Ibid.*, entry 1 June 1880; also Oxenham, *Memoir*, pp.99-108.

By the time the *Shannon* sailed down to Arica, arriving on 1 July 1880, the Chileans had already taken Tacna, the capital of the province, and had stormed the port. De Lisle declared that, although the Bolivian troops had fought well, the Peruvians had broken ranks and fled, adding, 'The Bolivians were utterly disgusted with their allies and declared they would fight no more with them and quietly disbanded and returned to La Paz and the interior'. However, he did admit that the Peruvian commander, Colonel Francisco Bolognesi, had fought gallantly and died resisting the enemy. He also noted that the Chileans were inclined to butcher wounded Peruvians rather than take prisoners. On 30 October, the *Shannon* once more anchored outside Callao, amidst the growing number of neutral warships, who had assembled in anticipation of the expected Chilean assault on Lima. On 23 November de Lisle noted the arrival of the *Christoforo Colombo,* the Italian flagship, which was built of wood with iron keels and thus able to move under steam at the rate of 17 knots, albeit not for long periods of time which, since she only carried relatively light guns, gave her 'always the advantage of being able to run away if necessary'. On 11 December he reported that the *Angamos* had fallen silent after its great gun burst loose from its stand and fell into the sea. Since Clements Markham later wrote that, 'No English ship in the Pacific Squadron equalled the *Angamos* either in speed or length of range', its disablement diminished the possibility of Chilean resistance to British diplomatic pressure.[17]

The Delivery of Lima

On 19 November 1880, the first division of a Chilean expeditionary force landed at the port of Pisco, south of Lima, soon to be followed by the landing of the remainder of the army further north at Curayaco Bay, near Lurín. In all, the invaders comprised 26,158 men, among whom there were 1,392 cavalry and 1,584 artillery men.[18] When Rear Admiral Frederick H. Stirling arrived in the *Triumph* at Callao on 21 November, he at once convoked a meeting on board his flagship of the senior officers of the British, French, Italian, German and American warships (Rear Admiral du Petit Thouars did not arrive aboard the *Victorieuse* until 7 January), and

---

17   *Ibid.*, entries 1-7 July, 23 November, 11 December 1880. On the *Angamos* see Markham, *The War between Peru and Chile*, pp.218-20, where he states that it was originally 'an Irish pig-boat named the *Belle of Cork*'.
18   Markham, *The War between Peru and Chile*, pp.227-38.

obtained their agreement to despatch naval officers as neutral observers to accompany the Chilean and Peruvian forces and, if necessary, to report any breach of the rules of war. Only the Germans chose not to participate in this delicate operation. Once permission was granted by President Nicolás de Piérola and General Manuel Baquedano, William Dyke Acland, commander of the *Triumph*, accompanied by an Italian, a French and an American officer, sailed to Pisco and joined the Chilean force on 29 November. By contrast, it was not until 22 December that Lieutenant Carey Brenton of the *Triumph*, also accompanied by three officers of the same nations, joined the Peruvian forces that were about to march to the battlefront. Both the British observers wrote frank reports about their assignments and Acland later published a revised account of his experience. Neither man spoke Spanish; but whereas Acland found that several Chilean officers spoke English, not to mention French, Brenton relied on Count Royck of the Italian Navy and Lieutenant Roberjot of the French Navy, who both spoke Spanish, to act as his interpreters.[19]

If we examine the reports of the two Englishmen, it becomes relatively easy to understand the causes of the Chilean victory. Acland found that the senior officers he dealt with were mainly men of substance and education who had volunteered and who led regiments that had been recruited in particular districts or occupations. There was a regiment recruited among the miners of Atacama and another from the port of Valparaíso; other units were raised from the tenantry of the haciendas. The soldiers impressed him as robust, disciplined and well equipped, albeit, when possible, much given to drink. All spoke a form of Spanish. Moreover, during the march from Pisco and still more, during their encampment at Lurín, the troops were drilled and trained in assault tactics. Their officers led from the front and indeed were to suffer heavy casualties.[20] By contrast, Brenton marvelled at the tardy manner in which the Peruvians prepared their defences and how ill-planned was their advance to the front. Moreover, if their senior officers sprang from the creole elite who governed the country, the lower officers, captains and below, appeared to Brenton to be virtually indistinguishable from the men in the ranks, who were mainly composed of Quechua-speaking Indians levied and brought down from the highlands. Many soldiers and even lower officers had little idea as to the significance of the forthcoming battle. Worse still, it was an army that lacked central command since, although Piérola had proclaimed himself commander-in-chief, he had no idea of how to conduct a battle.

---

19   For Stirling's *Letter to the Admiralty*, 18 February 1881, see Celia Wu-Brading, *Testimonios británicos*, pp.127-29. Note that the British reports printed in Spanish translation in *Testimonios* are to be found in The National Archives, Public Record Office, Foreign Office 61/337, and also in War Office 33/36, Papers 1881, Part I.
20   *Testimonios*, report of W.D. Acland, 27 January 1881, pp.51-52, 66-7.

The result was that each division fought alone, without coordination. Furthermore, the Peruvian army, when compared to the Chilean, was poorly armed, lacked adequate training, and was deficient in artillery and cavalry.[21]

In his subsequent report, Admiral Stirling noted that he had arranged to meet Admiral du Petit Thouars in Lima in the afternoon of 12 January and hence opted to spend the night in the British Legation, where he was welcomed by the Minister, Spenser St John, a diplomat of distinction with much experience in the Far East. Early on the morning of Thursday, 13 January 1881, news arrived that the battle for Lima had begun and, at the suggestion of St John, Stirling decided to remain in the Legation, which almost immediately opened its doors to refugees, to the point where it housed no less than 600 'women and children of all classes, colours and nationalities'. Stirling ordered Lieutenants de Lisle and Horsley to join him immediately in the Legation. It was thus thanks to his presence in Lima in an official capacity that de Lisle was able to provide such a vivid, first-hand account of the battles and the disturbances in Lima, adding striking details not to be found elsewhere. But he also used his skill to draw a remarkable and, at times, gruesome set of sketches of the battlefield and its combatants. In effect, de Lisle rose to the occasion and by pen and brush portrayed an axial moment in the history of South America.[22]

In his sketch-map of the battlefield, which he drew at the request of Lieutenant Carey Brenton, de Lisle depicted the two lines of the Peruvian defence, the first about six or eight miles long, stretched between the two towns of San Juan and Chorrillos, and the second, directly behind the first, comprised a series of armed redoubts in front of the town of Miraflores, some four miles in length. In his journal, de Lisle estimated the Peruvian army at 30,000, of which 8,000 were stationed in the Miraflores fortifications. He claimed that many Peruvian officers had slipped back for sleep and breakfast in Lima and hence were not present when the Chileans attacked early in the morning at 4 or 5 am. Although artillery and cavalry were brought into play, the Chileans won the day by frontal charges of their infantry. The only fierce resistance occurred at the Morro Solar, a hill outside Chorrillos, where the Peruvians used a Gatling gun to destroy their attackers. In general, however, de Lisle and the other British observers all agreed that once the Chileans drew close to the enemy lines, the Peruvians simply fled. He wrote, 'Generally speaking it may be said that most Peruvians bolted when their enemy got within 3 or 400 yards'. By then, of

---

21 *Ibid.*, report of R. Carey Brenton, 19 January 1881, pp.91-7, 105-07; he added 'I also noticed...how utterly the Peruvian army lacked one distinct head from whom all general orders ought to be originated and to whom all matters of general interest ought to have been reported.'.
22 *Testimonios*, Report of Rear Admiral Stirling, 31 March 1881, pp.131-32.

course, it was well known that the Chileans took few prisoners and bayoneted the wounded.[23]

With victory achieved and the Peruvians withdrawn to the Miraflores line, the Chileans took possession of the pleasant little town of Chorrillos and, after some hard fighting, proceeded to destroy the entire place. The most vivid description of the scenes that followed was provided by Commander Acland in his published account:

> Soon after the fighting was over, the troops broke into the grog shops and wine cellars, getting rapidly drunk, and becoming entirely out of control, and there ensued a scene of destruction and horror that I hope has rarely been witnessed in modern times; houses and property destroyed, men quarrelling and shooting each other for amusement, women violated, innocent civilians of any age murdered. The cemetery turned into a place where drunken soldiers held their orgies and even broke open the graves in order that the corpses might be removed to make way for their own drunken companions.

Among the victims was an Englishman, Dr Maclean, an old physician who had remained in the British Minister's house, confident in the protection of the British flag that adorned the building.[24] De Lisle repeated Acland's opinion that had the Peruvians counter-attacked that night of the 13 January, the Chilean army might well have been forced into retreat. As it was, the Chilean command used the next day, Friday, 14 January, to bring its troops to order and prepare for the assault on Miraflores. General Baquedano sent Colonel Miguel Iglesias, who had been captured with some 2,000 men during the previous day, back to Lima to convey the Chilean demand for the unconditional surrender of Lima and the Peruvian army. Close to midnight of that day, Acland was surprised to see Lieutenant Brenton and his Italian companion, Count Royck, arrive and seek an interview with Baquedano. He took the opportunity to impress upon Brenton the scale of the destruction of Chorrillos and begged him warn the British Minister of the danger to all women and children in Lima were the Chileans to attack the city.[25]

To understand the sequence of events, it is necessary to have recourse to the subsequent report of Spenser St John who, on learning of the message conveyed by Iglesias, convoked the diplomatic corps and, in the evening of the 14th, spoke with Piérola to obtain his agreement to their seeking to arrange an armistice so that at least the foreign communities, their women and children, might be evacuated from the city. Once his agreement was forthcoming, he sent Brenton and Royck by train to see Baquedano. The General agreed to see the diplomats the next

---

23   de Lisle, *Journal*, entry 13 January 1881.
24   William Dyke Acland, *Six Weeks with the Chilian Army. Being a short account of a march from Pisco to Lima and of the attack on Lima* (Norfolk Island, 1881), p.35; de Lisle, *Journal*, entry 13 January 1881.
25   *Testimonios*, Carey Brenton's report, pp.116-17.

morning at 7 am and offered them safe conduct back to Lima. The following morning of Saturday the 15th at 5 am, Spenser St John convoked a meeting of the leading ministers and naval commanders at the British Legation to discuss how best to assure the safety and property of the foreign residents of Lima. But why did the British Minister take this initiative and why did the French acquiesce in his leadership? The reasons were later clearly explained by the French Minister in his report to Paris in which he noted that, although in Peru France enjoyed a special influence both intellectual and commercial, in Chile, British ideas and capital predominated. It was hence best for French interests to accept the British lead, since their intervention 'will always have more weight than ours over the decisions of Chile'. Thus, when Admiral Stirling bluntly declared at the early morning meeting at the British Legation that if the Chileans, on entering Lima, attacked the Legations or neutral residents he would be obliged 'to take or sink the Chilean fleet', he was immediately supported by Rear Admiral du Petit Thouars and by Commodore Labrano of the Italian navy. In effect, the diplomatic corps thereby could, if necessary, advance a potent menace since, without a navy, the Chilean expeditionary force would be left isolated, deprived of support from its home base.[26]

At six-thirty in the same morning of 15 January, the British Minister, the French Minister, and the Salvadorean Minister, Tezanos Pinto, the dean of the diplomatic corps, took the train to the Chilean encampment there to meet with General Baquedano, the Minister of War, General Vergara, and a political agent of the government. The Chileans announced in forthright tone that they were not prepared to accept any peace negotiations until Lima and Callao should unconditionally surrender. They did not regard the question of neutral property or lives as being of any real importance. Since de Vorges had asked St John, 'to take the more considerable share in the discussion'. The British Minister then informed the Chileans that he had been instructed by his government to take whatever measures necessary to protect British subjects and that he intended to act on those instructions. He warned that Rear Admiral Stirling and his officers were staying in the Legation to guarantee its security and, were anyone in the Legation to be injured, it would prove to be a grave misfortune for everyone concerned. The same was true for all the neutral citizens resident in Lima, since the diplomatic corps here acted as one. Although General Baquedano had said that neutral flags would be respected, in Chorrillos, St John's own house, which bore the flag of the British Legation, had been sacked and Dr Maclean, an old physician of seventy-seven, had been murdered within its walls. Given this occurrence, how could the

---

26   *Ibid.*, Report of Spenser St John to Earl Granville, 22 January 1881, pp.141-42. For the French support of the British initiatives, see letter of Eugene Domet de Vorges, *Testimonios*, pp.43-4.

diplomatic corps trust the word of Baquedano? Almost two hours were consumed in this discussion with de Vorges and St John advancing their arguments, since 'both of us decided to use every means before resorting to any direct threat'. After the Chileans had retired to consider the matter, Baquedano then returned alone and gave his word of honour that, if it was necessary to attack and take Miraflores, he would station cavalry to prevent his soldiers from entering Lima until the city had the opportunity of surrendering. At that point he would only occupy the city with a body of elite troops. In order to give the diplomats time to persuade Piérola to come to terms, Baquedano extended the armistice until midnight of that day.[27]

While these negotiations were in train, Admirals Stirling and du Petit Thouars, together with Commodore Labrano, visited the National Palace in Lima to obtain permission from the Foreign Minister, Pedro José Calderón, to use the trains leaving Lima to evacuate neutral residents and their women and children. But the Minister refused to take responsibility for the decision and arranged for them to take the train to Miraflores to see Piérola. On their interviewing the president, he immediately gave orders that all trains should be placed at the disposal of the evacuation of neutral citizens, women and children. The naval commanders remained in the house occupied by Piérola, which was only 200 to 300 yards away from the fortified front. There then arrived St John, de Vorges and other diplomats who had been invited to breakfast with Piérola for the purpose of discussing the terms on which peace could be negotiated. Barely had they sat down when they found themselves in the midst of a Chilean bombardment, not merely from the field artillery but also from the fleet stationed off the coast. Since it was too dangerous to return to the train, both diplomats and naval commanders were obliged to hurry across the fields which at that time still separated Miraflores from Lima.[28] In his journal, de Lisle, who obviously had accompanied Stirling, provided a lively impression of the spectacle,

> They were at breakfast when suddenly heavy firing took place, bullets etc flying all round them; there was immediately a rush, and away went Admirals, Ministers etc at full speed – the conference was at an end; it seemed as though the Chileans had broken faith and now wound up by attempting to murder the would-be Peace Makers. They all arrived in Lima smothered in dust but fortunately without damage, the French Admiral (du Petit Thouars) was nearly cut down by a Peruvian dragoon... The US Minister, Christiancy, arrived exceedingly limp, having run nearly all the way: coat torn, shirt unbuttoned: the French Minister very much washed out and fuming at the unseemly interruption, the

---

27   *Ibid.*, pp.142-44.
28   *Ibid.*, Stirling's report, pp.134-36.

German ditto, nearly fainted and had to be assisted by the French flag lieutenant, who supported him in his arms; he arrived hardly recognisable, hat knocked in, livid and in a fainting condition… Mr St John (Spenser) and the British Admiral arrived in the best condition of all: very dusty, coats flying away, but still ready to run another mile if necessary…

De Lisle added that the rumour spread quickly that Stirling had been killed and that a messenger took the news to Ancón, so that orders were given at once for *Triumph* and *Victorieuse* to be cleared for action, albeit soon to be withdrawn once a telegram arrived stating that all was well.[29]

What had happened, so it was later concluded, was that General Baquedano and his staff had sallied forth to reconnoitre the terrain before Miraflores and, by mistake, had approached too close to the Peruvian lines, whose defenders, despite the armistice, could not refrain from opening fire. The Chilean response was almost immediate. The battle lasted for almost four hours and was hard fought, since the Peruvians had constructed a series of redoubts which had to be taken by the frontal attack of the Chilean infantry. Although both de Lisle and Brenton commented on the Peruvian soldiers quitting the battle while shouting '*Viva el Perú*', the losses on the Chilean side were considerable, evidence that not all the defenders simply 'bolted' when the enemy drew near. Indeed, de Lisle heard that some forty per cent of Chilean officers were killed or wounded in the two battles for Lima. Whatever the case, by the evening, the Peruvian army had abandoned the field of battle and effectively disappeared from sight. De Lisle commented,

> The greater part of the Peruvian troops quietly disbanded during the night and started off for their native mountains without food or anything; numbers would die on the way, but the *rabonas* led the way prepared for hardships their husbands might be unable to endure.

Lieutenant Cary Brenton remained close to the battlefield until he could be sure that the Chilean troops did not seek to enter Lima. He then returned to the Legation to inform Admiral Stirling of that fact and, after observing Peruvian officers changing into civilian clothes, he said farewell to Colonel Andrés Avelino Cáceres, who had been wounded in the leg as he sought in vain to rally his troops.[30]

The evacuation of foreign residents and their women and children by train to the seaside resort of Ancón took place on the 15th while the battle of Miraflores was being fought. The

---

29   de Lisle, *Journal*, entry 15 January 1881.
30   *Testimonios*, Carey Brenton's report, pp.119-21.

scenes of confusion were inevitable, since rumour abounded and there was a general fear that Lima might be subjected to the destruction wrought on Chorrillos, Barranco and Miraflores. A further rumour was that Peruvian deserters might come down to Ancón with the purpose of plundering the refugees. It was to restore order and avert these fears that Captain D'Arcy of the *Shannon* called a meeting of neutral warship captains, who agreed each to land a number of marines and sailors to guard the town. During the night of Sunday the 16th, the mob of the capital broke loose and began to attack property. Whether there were many ex-soldiers in among the rioters is not at all clear. When de Lisle mentioned the fires, he blamed the African or mulatto sector of the population for the outrage. Whatever the case, he commented,

> The night of the 15 January will long be remembered with shame by the Peruvians. Their own people attempted to burn Lima and then sack it, and actually succeeded in part, for at one time Lima was burning in three places: the whole of the Chinese quarter was destroyed and sacked, the unhappy Chinese murdered; and anyone who ventured into the streets was received with a shower of bullets.

Since de Lisle was subsequently made an honorary member of the Fire Brigade of Lima 'in recognition of the energy and courage he displayed in helping to rescue the sufferers and extinguish the flames', he obviously spent a great deal of that night engaged in the preservation of the city. In the early morning of Monday, 17 January, Captain de Champeaux, an elderly Frenchman, a veteran of the Imperial Guard, assembled the Foreign Urban Guard, procured arms from the *Alcalde* and then authorised its members to shoot at discretion all rioters who remained on the streets. While this new tragedy unfolded, the Peruvian navy blew up the remainder of its ships that remained in the harbour of Callao.[31]

Once the British, French and Italian ministers and naval commanders had regained their composure following their flight from Miraflores, that same night of the 15th they entered the national palace to enquire of Calderón, the Foreign Minister, the whereabouts of Piérola, so as to arrange the terms of surrender. But on finding him unhelpful, they decided to take the matter in their own hands and located the *alcalde* or Mayor of Lima, Rufino Torrico, who agreed to assume the responsibility of offering the unconditional surrender of the city, provided that his interview with General Baquedano was witnessed by the British, French and Italian ministers and naval commanders. It may be noted that, although de Lisle was present during these negotiations, the pages of his journal recording the events have been lost. At 11 pm on the 15th,

---

31 de Lisle, *Journal*, entries 15 and 16 January. Note that all other sources agree that the main riot occurred on the night of Sunday, 16 January.

Lieutenant Brenton, together with Lieutenants Conde Royck and Roberjot, was ordered by Stirling to go by special train to see Baquedano. Their arrival in Chorrillos proved unwelcome to the Chileans, who had suffered severe casualties during the battle for Miraflores. Brenton was obliged to wait until the morning to receive a letter from the Chilean General to take to the British Legation. On the morning of Sunday the 16th, the ministers, naval commanders and Torrico went by train to Chorrillos and there the terms of unconditional surrender of Lima were signed by all parties present. On Monday afternoon, well after the Foreign Urban Guard had restored order to the streets of the capital, the first detachment of the Chilean army entered Lima and, on the following day, General Baquedano and his men proudly paraded through the streets of Lima.[32]

In *The War between Peru and Chile 1878-1882* (1882), Sir Clements R. Markham, a former naval officer who had travelled extensively in Peru and who was later to be an influential president of the Royal Geographical Society, argued that, if the Peruvians abandoned their fortified line at Miraflores after four hours of battle, it was because their supply of ammunition was exhausted. He added, 'Surely the slander that the Peruvians will not fight bravely for their country and die for it ought to be silenced before these facts'. Drawing upon the recently published account of the war written by Benjamin Vicuña Mackenna, a leading Chilean historian and politician, he stated that, in the two battles for Lima, Chilean casualties were 5,443, of whom 1,299 were killed and 4,144 wounded. With the collapse of the Peruvian state, no accurate figures of fatalities can be provided, even if Markham estimated 6,000 deaths and 3,000 wounded. As for the fate of Lima, he affirmed, 'Its rescue from destruction is due to the firm stand made by the British Minister Sir Spenser St John, backed by the material power and firm resolve of the English and French Admirals'.[33] But, although Lima was peacefully occupied, its inhabitants did not escape punitive measures since, as Clements Markham observed, not only were the Chileans, 'harsh and exacting, but they pushed their power of appropriating and confiscating to unprecedented lengths…'. It was not until 20 October 1883 that the Peace Treaty of Ancón was signed, in which Peru was obliged to cede permanent possession of the province of Tarapacá and allow the Chilean occupation of the province of Tacna and Arica.[34]

As for Rudolph de Lisle, he sailed back to England on HMS *Shannon*, arriving in Devonport in July 1881, after a cruise of more than two years. He took advantage of his time in England to

---

32 *Testimonios*, Reports of St John and Stirling, pp.136-7, 144-45.
33 Markham, *The War between Peru and Chile*, pp.258, 60.
34 Markham, *The War*, pp.260, 268.

attend a course at Greenwich on gunnery and torpedoes. In 1883 he was sent for service in the Mediterranean, where in the previous year the British navy had bombarded the forts of Alexandria and a British army, numbering 14,400 men, defeated the nationalist regime of Arabi Pasha, thereby allowing an informal British protectorate over Egypt to be installed. But at once the occupying power was confronted with the problem of the Sudan, where a Muslim messianic movement, led by the Mahdi, had arisen. The British agent in Khartoum, General Charles Gordon, was surrounded and besieged, thereby impelling the government to despatch an expeditionary force to rescue him. Among the forces sent up the Nile was a naval brigade commanded by Lord Charles Beresford, and among its officers was Rudolph de Lisle. At this time, promotion in the Victorian navy was slow and difficult and hence navy officers greeted the opportunity of winning distinction in land operations with enthusiasm. It was on 17 January 1885, at the battle of Abu Klea, relatively close to Khartoum, that 2,000 British troops, the naval brigade among them, were surprised by some 10,000 followers of the Mahdi. In that battle Rudolph de Lisle was killed, some two months after his 32nd birthday. His clerical Victorian biographer declared, 'Thus he fell, like his Crusader ancestor of old, like his brother Everard in the Indian Mutiny – for he too was slain by the armed devotees of the false Prophet – against the enemies of England and the faith'.[35] A requiem mass was celebrated in the Cistercian abbey church of Mount St Bernard founded by his father some fifty years before, where his brief life and many virtues were duly celebrated.

---

35 Oxenham, *Memoir*, pp.220-34, 242.

Gibraltar

Channel Squadron leaving Malta

Smyrna.

HMS Minotaur bearing the Flag of Lord John Hay (left) with HMS Shannon (centre)
and HMS Invincible (right).

he diary begins on 24 April 1878 when Rudolph joins HMS *Prince Albert*; commissioned by Captain Loftus Jones at Devonport and launched in 1864 at a cost of £215,158.

On 27 December 1878, he joined HMS *Himalaya* and they sailed from Portsmouth to Malta (via Gibraltar) where, on 13 January 1879, he joined HMS *Shannon* (1875) whose commander was Captain W Burley Grant. They spend the following months exercising and occasionally shooting snipe woodcocks etc. in the Ottoman empire of Turkey, such as at Smyrna and Vourlah, and sailed to Cyprus and back to Malta.

They anchored in Syracuse Harbour on 9 May 1879, went past the active volcano of Stromboli on 18 May, and reached Naples on 30 May, having sighted Vesuvius the night before. Rudolph then goes to Rome on four days' leave 'with 5 of our fellows and had a most enjoyable visit' staying at the Hotel d'Angleterre.

High mass at St Peter's was 'a grand service… the singing very good… and glad to say Gregorian just the same as we used to have at Garendon'. He returns to Naples and they reached Port Mahon, Menorca, on 23 January arriving at Gibraltar on 1 July. On 18 July, they are informed that, instead of going back to Plymouth, England, they are to sail to Valparaiso – 'You are ordered to Pacific'.

They reached Madeira on 23 July and their new commander was Captain John D'Arcy. Rudolph enjoyed Funchal, 'A more agreeable ten days I haven't spent for a long time' and he draws a very accurate map of their trip from Spain to Brazil. They finally reached Rio de Janeiro on 29 August 1879.

We will begin to follow his progress around South America, which will end in January 1881 in Peru.

Rudolph and a friend sketching above Rio.

View of the Corcovado, Rio de Janeiro from the Anchorage.

1879

aving had a delightful visit to Madeira, coaled etc; we sailed on the 2 August at 6 pm.

3 August   11 pm a fine fair breeze stopped engines made plain sail.

11 August   We sighted S Antonio, the wind becoming variable with heavy rain.

12 August   The wind veered round to the WSW.

14/15 August   The weather squally with heavy rain, 5-7 from the westward veering to SSW.

17 August   And gradually round to SSE.

19 August   Crossed the line in Longitude 25°38'W. The weather was fine all the way from the line to Rio de Janeiro[1] where we arrived on the 19th, having had a very good passage.

29 August   Had a very good passage. Once a week we had Penny Readings etc. and twice theatricals, once by the officers and the second time by the Ship's Company. The former piece 'The Irish Tutor' in which Messrs Ponsonby[2] and Somerville[3] specially distinguished themselves.

---

1   Then capital of Brazil.
2   Lieutenant Henry, HMS *Shannon*.
3   Lieutenant, HMS *Shannon*.

Ink drawing of Rio woodscape.

Found here HMS *Gannet*[4], Italian frigate *Garibaldi*[5], the Brazilian fleet looking dirtier and more disorganised than ever. This glorious harbour looked grander and more picturesque than ever, the beautiful outline of the hills, the Corcovado and Tifuca Peaks towering above the others, the head of the harbour dotted with islands or rather their mirage, and lost in the distance of blue hill and sky. The city situated upon gently sloping hills; the churches being the most prominent buildings visible, always excepting the hideous barracks. Near the Sugar Loaf, the hills are all covered with the most gorgeous trees, the foliage of which are so dense, that in many places the sun's rays never penetrate.

The walk up the Corcovado[6] is a delightful one, good road easy ascent in the shade nearly all the way, beautiful woodland scenery and a splendid view from the summit of the whole harbour. The ascent of the Sugar Loaf is the thing to do, but I was never able to get a boat, and one has to wait for a perfectly smooth day as one has to land from outside.

Tifuca is a most charming place, distant about nine miles from Rio, and is reached by tramway or the greater part of the distance, but there is always a diligence waiting to take one to White's Hotel, which is situated at the head of the gorge, in the most enchanting scenery of rock, mountain and luxuriant vegetation.

There is also a beautiful waterfall just above the hotel, well worth seeing; below is a delightful pool, or rather swimming bath of icy cold water, completely shaded from the sun, and at all times most inviting; a plunge into this deliciously cool bath after a walk is most refreshing. The 'doings' at the hotel are good, as also the accommodation, but what specially made it attractive to the officers of the *Shannon* was its 'Birds Nest' of the Botanical Gardens, with its celebrated avenue of palm trees, superb specimens but rather monotonous owing to their exact similarity, it is needless to speak. But the flowers were fully appreciated and especially after a long cruise for us. The butterflies are plentiful and of many fine and rare varieties, and are cheap when bought in a case

---

4   British Sloop, 1878, built Sheerness, England (1137 tons, 1100 HP).
5   Italian Frigate, built 1860, retired 1894.
6   'View of the Corcovado, Rio de Janeiro from the Anchorage' see picture p.38.

complete. Rio is specially renowned for its feather flowers and different varieties of beetles etc. These latter make pretty bracelets or necklaces.

The streets are fairly well paved, and in some of the principal streets, a wood pavement is being laid down. Trams intersect the whole place, and are well conducted besides being most convenient. At this time of the year, the place is sickly, and a good deal of the yellow fever exists, so much so, that I was unable to obtain leave to go snipe shooting about twenty miles inland. As it was, one of our men[7] caught it, and succumbed a few days later, before our arrival at Montevideo, fortunately the weather was cool, or the infection might have spread in the ship.

The Italian frigate *Garibaldi* had sprung her mainyard before her arrival, and she took a day to hoist her new one in, and never even attempted to rig a derrick. She had double topsail yards and is a vessel of the year I, but these Italians frigates are not very plentiful, though they (Italians) are a first class power? Or wish so to be thought and treated.

7/8 September   The weather on the 7th and 8th was bad, and steamers coming in from the southward reported foul weather outside, so the Captain decided to remain, which we did until the 9th (September).

9 September   He gave a dance on board which proved to be a great success; there were a large number of people on board amongst them a sprinkling of foreign officers. The US frigate *Hartford*[8] was laying in the harbour, and a smart looking vessel she seemed, in appearance anyway. One of the drawbacks of Rio is the absence of water, which is supplied by an aquaduct from the Corcovado, but the drainage is bad, chiefly I fancy owing to want of water, and to this cause, fevers no doubt may be attributed.

10 September   Went to sea and found a heavy head swell, but no wind showing, plainly we had been wise in remaining two days longer in harbour than we had intended.

---

7   Thomas Gowman, stoker, died of it on 14 September 1879, HMS *Shannon*.
8   American Frigate. Built Boston, USA, 1858, Norfolk USA Navy Yard. Sunk at her berth 1956. 2900 tons.

14 September   Thomas Gowman (Stoker) died and was committed to the deep. No other cases of yellow fever. The weather perfect and rapidly cooling, the sea smooth, making our way down under steam, sail now being found a valuable auxiliary to steam, instead of vice versa as was originally intended.

15 September   1 am. Weather very thick. Slowly wound our way up to anchorage off Montevideo,[9] but when fog lifted, found ourselves a long way from the town, weighed and shifted further in fourteen fathoms; we were of course at once put in quarantine and had to ship down the river to Flores Island[10] a miserable place with a hospital upon it.

   The *Avon* was at Montevideo, which was a good thing, as her captain took a good deal of trouble in seeing provisions, coal etc., forwarded to us. So full of infection were we (or supposed to be), that the officials strewed disinfectants where our men had stood in the coal lighters.

16 September   The *Garibaldi* passed on her way to Montevideo, our anchorage was in 11¾ fathoms.

   Sheep, cattle etc. are of course very cheap here, in fact, including the cost of transit to Flores, sheep were one third of what they were at Rio, and much better.

18 September   Having received 210 tons of coal, at 9.20 we weighed and proceeded, beautiful weather as usual; sounded upon the English bank. Found neither tide nor current.

25 September   Observed Cape Virgins. 7.50 pm anchored off Dungeness[11] in twelve fathoms; ebb tide, but a sandy bottom. The beacon showed out very distinctly and clearly. The weather all the way from Flores was perfect. The sea smooth and nice cool winds, a slight contrast to what we had expected.

---

9   Capital of Uruguay. Population 250,000 (1977); 1,350,000 (2005).
10 In middle of the channel of Rio de la Plata.
11 Mainland point at entrance to Magellan Strait.

HMS Gannet.

26 September   Weighed and proceeded along the north shore steaming for the entrance to the 1st Narrows; we reached this point at 3 pm, expecting this time to be the first of the flood but practically in slack water. After leaving Cape Porscone, keep it bearing right astern until you make out direction, should you fail to see this mark owing to the thickness or badness of the weather, return at once and wait for a more favourable opportunity. Anchored in Gregory Bay, nine fathoms,, but unfortunately so late that we could not land. A farm is the only building visible, the land well wooded land and low, and a renowned place for Guanaco shooting.

27 September   Left Gregory Bay at daylight and steamed through 2nd Narrows and New Channel; we were steaming eight knots in the Narrows and tide running about eight miles an hour with us. When steering for New Channel, keep the Cone open from Cape St Vincent[12] or if it is not visible, Gregory Shoulder will equally do. Anchored off Sandy Point in thirteen fathoms; sand and mud, it is not advisable to anchor in less than ten fathoms. The beacon on Sandy Point has disappeared but there is a hut (white) still there. At this place, the weather suddenly changed, coming on in a violent gush with snow and sleet squalls and we soon found the *Shannon* weather was at an end for the Straits anyhow. A more desolate place it is hardly possible to conceive, a poverty stricken looking place built of wood, no hills near it to relieve its monotony, but ground covered with half dead trees and snow. To the right of the town is marshy ground, but little to be got out of it. We succeeded in getting however, a few duck and teal and two very fine geese of beautiful plumage. There are a great many Ibis about and most delicious eating they are, but this fact was discovered rather late, though we secured several. The exports seem to be Guanaco skins and the robes made of them are exceedingly handsome, and very cheap, £2 or so. When at Arica[14], or some other places where these animals are to be found in sufficient numbers, the price of a robe is £10 or

---

12   Actually on an island in the Strait or another Cape south-east of the island of Tierra del Fuego.
13   Named after Fernando de Magellan (1470-1521) who sailed through this strait in 1520. Rudolph appears to have been in this area several times between 1870 and 1881.
14   City of Peru captured (and retained) by Chile in 1879, nearly 1,000 miles from Lima.

HMS Shannon passing Thornton Peaks.

£15. Coal can now be had, an enterprising German firm having established a depot at this out of the way place, but no doubt with an eye to the main chance.

29 September Left Sandy Point at 8.20 am, the weather having completely changed, quite warm and sunny. Met HMS *Opal,* homeward bound off Port Famine; at 4.45 pm anchored in S Nicholas Bay in 11½ fathoms.

Sent a shoring party away, and got a very good haul of fish – a party of officers went away up the river shooting, saw a woodcock, but we didn't secure it.

30 September   ...weighed at midnight and proceeded through the various reaches, the scenery rapidly becoming finer, all the hills snow capped and rugged. Passed several glaciers, the wind west, cold and rapidly increasing with driving squalls of sleet. The weather becoming rapidly thicker and threatening. Went into Port Angosto, a beautifully

HMS Shannon outward bound passing a glacier, Straits of Magellan.

land locked harbour with a narrow and circuitous entrance, with just room for one ship, the harbour being shaped like a cup with high hills all round the lower portions covered with trees and jungle the upper part; the monotony of the rock only broken by yellow moss, and in innumerable rivulets running down the steep face of the cliffs. There was however, one beautiful waterfall, but no signs of any Indians or dwelling of any other description; we noticed several kelp, geese and a good number of 'Steamer' duck but of course they are worthless. We anchored in the centre of the basin in fifteen fathoms. Anchors between 3rd point and SW Waterfall, 98°20' and 3rd point and Hay Point 62°32'.

It poured with rain all the time, but this it seems to do when once one arrives as far to the westward as Sandy Point.

1 October   Left and proceeded through Sea Reach. Weather very thick and dirty, with a fast falling barometer made for Port Churruca, and anchored in Nassau anchorage in 15½ fathoms, sand and rock. The entrance is narrow, and for a ship of this size difficult, but then she turns so perfectly that she could go anywhere almost. The scenery is much the same stamp as Angosto but grander, higher hills, more waterfalls, etc. The weather abominable.

2 October   Barometer inclined to rise, weighed at 8 am and proceeded for Cape Pillar, found both flukes of anchor gone, broken shorn off leaving 3½ feet on both arms. No doubt done by letting go upon a rock; found outside the weather thick and more threatening than ever, the squalls coming over the high hills in gusts with blinding snow; had to put back, but this time anchored in Oldfield Anchorage. A place very little better than the last, as far as the ground is concerned. In Nassau Anchorage, the place is more sheltered, but so very rocky that it is unadvisable to anchor there if it can be helped, and another objection is one is liable to drag down hill.

At Oldfield, one drags up hill, but there's so little room that, unless in very deep water, there is hardly room for one's stern to clear. When we anchored here first, the wind went down and once more we saw the sun; banked fires but very soon wanted our steam for down came a Willy-Waw, we tautened our cable and our stern swung not ten feet clear of the rocks, rather an anxious time; weighed and shifted berth further out and anchored in 28 fathoms.

The water perfectly white with the rushing squalls, steaming up to our anchors, towards night the wind falling, but still gusty, and the hills covered with snow. Barometer very low, 29.01; the wind veered to the south with squalls of snow and hail.

5 October   Barometer rising with SW wind and squalls of sleet. 5.50 am weighed and proceeded – at noon abreast of Cape Pillar, blowing hard and heavy sea running. Wind freshening. Barometer steady.

6 October   Strong westerly gale. 5.15 am eased engines and lay to our Port Tack with Forestaysail – ship drifting about 1½ knots an hour to leeward, but making very good weather. Barometer again falling extreme roll 25°. Heavy sea from the westward. This rolling satisfied several of us, for it was always hinted that in certain weather, the *Shannon* might not prove the best of sea boats, but she certainly belied these sinister hints and was wonderfully dry, but then it must be remembered she was only under forestaysail, and a portion of the time with main topsail set. The guns during the gale might have been fought perfectly well, when another ship could not have opened her ports.

7 October   Barometer lowest at 7 am viz: 29.04. Weather moderating, ship pitching heavily, put her jib-boom under also dipped stern boat. Got jib-boom in. 1 pm went round on Starboard Tack shaped course and proceeded thirty-six revolutions. Heavy swell from the westward. Weather rapidly moderating, but wind inclined to back to the NW.

8 October   5 am. Barometer 29.16, wind veering to the westward. Set fore and aft sails. Made sail to double reefed topsails and foresail.

9/10 October   Winds light with fine weather and rising barometer.

13 October   Light south-westward wind, sea smooth getting into Humbolt's[15] current.

---

15   Called after Alexander von Humbolt (1769-1859). Born in Berlin; naturalist and scientific writer..

View of the coast nearing Valparaiso. The white peaks of Aconcagua can be seen in the distance (left); the highest mountain in South America at a height of 23,474 ft. with the Bell of Guillota (central) and a distant view of the Andes (right).

Coquimbo, Chile. Nereus, hospital, church, Custom House, and Gannet can all be seen.

14 October   Wind steadily freshening from the SSW; all sail set.

15 October   Strong southerly wind with a following sea; stopped engines, making seven knots.

16 October   3.15 am. Drew fires forward and lay to under steam till daylight; furled sails and proceeded in for the land. 9.45 anchored in 33 fathoms and Valparaiso Bay[16] veered to seven shackles.

We remained at Valparaiso until the 21st when we sailed for Coquimbo.[17] We found in the former place, a perfect state of furore, on account of the capture of the Peruvian Monitor *Huascar*[18] by the Chilean fleet off Angamos Point.[19] All Santiago came to see the triumphant arrival of the ship. The only ship, or rather Ironclad which had participated in the fight, being the *Blanco Encalada,*[20] the *Almirante Cochrane*'s[21] sister ship. The *Cochrane* being away, all the cudos naturally was given to the *Blanco,* which ship was daily visited by crowds of people. Though she fired thirty-two at the *Huascar* she only hit her three times, and at 25 or 30 yards distance when trying to ram. One of her shots however did good execution, for it entered the *Cochrane*'s side abaft battery, and passed through the other side, the splinters however killing one and wounding ten men. The *Blanco* declare it was one of the *Huascar*'s shots, but not so the *Cochrane*.

The *Huascar,* until the time of her capture, had been the scare of the whole coast, of the Chileans especially, though they had two Ironclads carrying each six guns of twelve tons, and twice the thickness of armour. In fact, it is rumoured that before the final trap was laid, Mr Reed[22] telegraphed to enquire what had happened to the two vessels he had built.

16   Main sea port of Chile. Population: 109,000 (1877), 725,000 (1977), 900,000 (2005).
17   360 miles north of Santiago; one of the best sheltered harbours on the coast and winter quarters for Chilean Navy. Population: 65,000 (1977), 100,000 (2005).
18   Peruvian Ironclad, built in Britain in 1865, captured by the Chilians on 8 October 1879, tons 1130, 300 HP.
19   Forty miles north of Antofagasta.
20   Chilean Ironclad, built in Britain in 1875, flagship of Rear Admiral Galvarino Riveros (1830-1892), tons: 3560, 2920 HP.
21   Chilean Ironclad, built in Britain in 1875. Named after Admiral Thomas Cochrane (1775-1860) 1831, 10th Earl of Dundonald, Commander of Chilean Navy during war of Liberation. His third son Hon Arthur Cochrane (1824-1905) RN. 3560 tons, 2920 HP.
22   British engineer; probably of Hull (Markham 1883 p.93/4).

Track of HMS Shannon from Montevideo to Valparaiso from
18 September 1879 to 16 October 1879.

Blanco Encalada (Chilean), Union (Peruvian), Huascar (Peruvian Turret and Ram) and
Almirante Cochrane (Chilean) during the capture of the Huascar (Grau)
by the Chilean Ironclads Blanco and Cochrane.

Hearing the *Huascar* was cruising off Antofagasta,[23] the *Blanco, Covadonga*[24] and *Matias Cousino*[25] (armed transport) sailed south from Angamos, having previously arranged with the *Cochrane,* who was cruising some way to the westward, to cut off her retreat to the northward, and sighted the *Huascar* steering north with the *Union*[26] (Corvette). No sooner did the *Huascar* make out the *Blanco,* than she steered onto the westward, the *Blanco* steering to cut her off from the instant retreat north. The *Huascar* had got as far north as Angamos Point, when the smoke was distinctly made out of three other vessels bearing north-west. The *Huascar* now put on all steam, and began to creep away from the *Blanco,* who had never come within gunshot. The *Union* made off at full speed followed by the *Covadonga.*

The *Cochrane* steered to cut off the *Huascar* which she did and opened fire at 2,000 yards; the *Huascar* having fired a couple of shots at 4,000 yards first. The distance rapidly decreased and the firing becoming general. The *Cochrane* fired forty-five shots (Palliser shells[27]). The *Huascar's* tower was pierced early in the action and Grau,[28] her commander, killed; his body was never recovered. The steering gear disabled, her turret pierced in two places, one shell killing and wounding everyone inside. After Grau's death the action was practically over for the *Blanco* had now arrived, and began firing away and the unfortunate *Huascar* was turned into a slaughter house.

She lost 25 killed and 113 wounded. Most of her men were killed manoeuvring the relieving tackles, after the steering gear had been cut.

The extraordinary thing is, that neither of the Chileans were able to ram the *Huascar* when she lay a helpless toy upon the water, but simply lay off and pounded her. With her captain, 1st, 2nd and 3rd lieutenants killed, steering gear disabled, and pouring an incessant fire upon her decks, so much so, that no one could show his head on deck without being shot, once the colours were down, or the Chileans say so, but the *Huascar* was simply running at full speed, so they ranged up again and opened fire.

---

23 576 miles north of Valparaiso.
24 Chilean sloop built ?, 600 tons, 140 HP, sunk Chancay Bay, Peru, 13 September 1880.
25 Chilean Transport.
26 Peruvian Corvette built France 1864. 1150 tons, 400 HP, scuttled Callao, 16 January 1881.
27 Invented by Sir William Palliser (1830-1882).
28 Almirante Miguel Grau (1834-1879): Flagship *Huascar.*

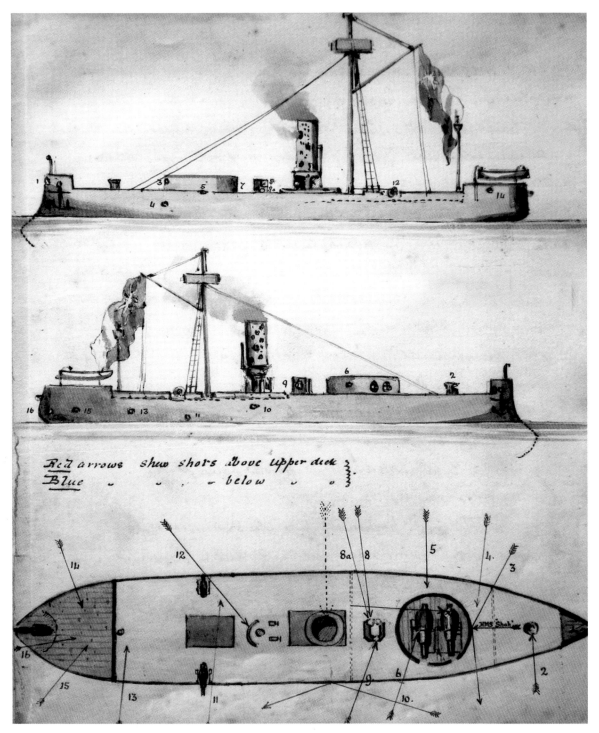

Red arrows shew shors above upper deck
Blue ⁓ ⁓ ⁓ ⁓ below ⁓ ⁓ ⁓

Huascar, late Peruvian Monitor.

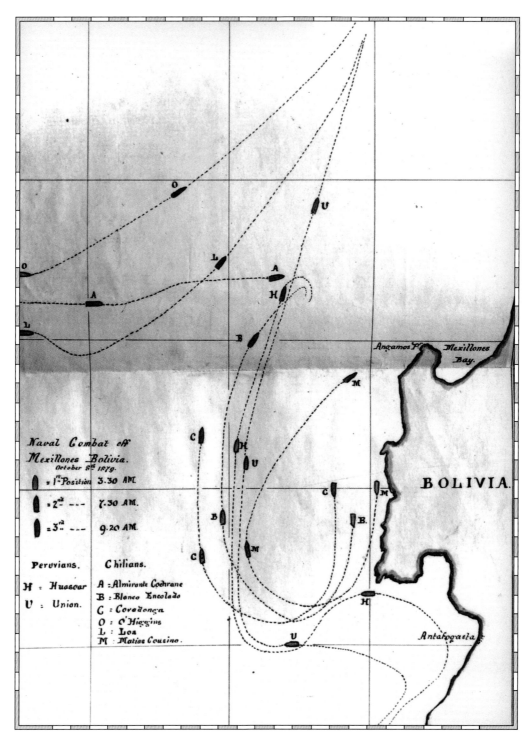

Naval combat off Mexillones, Bolivia, 8 October 1879.[29]

At last engines were stopped, colours hauled down, and a boat took possession and hoisted Chilean colours. The *Union* had been chased by the *O'Higgins*[30] and *Loa*,[31] but the latter vessel, being much faster than the other, soon distanced her, so that *Union*, had she been so willing, might have turned round and taken both vessels in detail, but she made use of her super speed to retreat to Arica with the news. The little *Covadonga* arrived in time to have a solitary shot at the *Huascar*. The latter ship was set on fire during the action but the flames were easily extinguished after she had been boarded. Though so much knocked about, her engines were intact, her turret could be revolved and her guns worked; her armament consisted of two 10 inch Armstrong[32] muzzle loading guns firing 300 lb projectiles, also two 40 pounders on the lower deck, one of which had the case taken off by one of the *Cochrane*'s shots, and one 20 pounders aft. Her armour on the turret, $5\frac{1}{2}$ x 13 inch teak backing, and an inner skin of 2 x $\frac{1}{2}$ inch plates. The conning tower was protected by three inch iron and nine inch teak, and not even rounded off. It was utterly destroyed. Ship's side protected by $4\frac{1}{2}$ tapering to $2\frac{1}{2}$ at the bow and stern, with $2\frac{1}{2}$ inch plates inner skin.

The *Union* carried twelve 40 pounder guns, with a speed of 13 or 14 knots.

The *Cochrane* and *Blanco* were very formidable vessels of their size, twin screws, central battery, carrying six 12 ton guns. This protected by 7 inch armour, tapering to 6 inch, and protected at the waterline by 9 inch armour, tapering to $5\frac{1}{2}$.

O'Higgins corvette of wood, carrying seven 40 pounders, speed about ten knots.

Covadonga sloop carrying five guns.

The two armed transports *Loa* and *Matias Cousino*.

During action *Cochrane* fired forty-five Palliser shells. In addition to being struck by the *Blanco*, she was struck on the starboard bow near the waterline, the shell knocking her galley to pieces and killing one man. This unequal combat lasted $1\frac{1}{2}$ hours.

When the *Huascar* arrived on the 20th, the bay was very gay with the number of

---

29 Mexillones, Bolivia. This is now part of Chile and is 40 miles north of Antofagasta. Bolivia would still have a port or passage to the Pacific Ocean. It lost its Pacific Coast during the 1879/1881 war. Population 540 (1876), 5,000 (1977). See map page 58.
30 Chilean Corvette built 1867, 1670 tons, 800 HP.
31 Chilean Transport, sunk Callao, Peru, 22 March 1880.
32 Invented by Sir (Lord) William Armstrong (1810-1900). Rifle-bore breech-loading gun with cylinder.

boats dotted about and prepared to escort her in. The batteries saluted as she arrived, but the people at large were disappointed, with her thinking she was at least as large as the *Cochrane*. Great numbers of people came on board, so as to get a good view of her, and we improved the occasion by having an impromptu dance, and did the cure to such an extent, that numbers came off next day to see the ship. We had dancing twice, and found the Chilean ladies had not deteriorated in appearance. I found several of my old friends, amongst others the Serrateas[33] in great form and as kind as ever and as hospitable, made several new acquaintances at their house.

21 October   Left Valparaiso for Coquimbo.[34] Moderate SW winds made all plainsail.

22 October   7 am. Stopped engines.

23 October   4 am. Commenced steam. 8 am furled sails. 11.45 am anchored in Coquimbo Bay in 14½ fathoms, veered to 4 shackles. Found here *Liffey*[35] store ship, US Flagship *Pensacola*[36] (Rear Admiral Rodgers[37]). Stayed here until the 28th when we were ordered off by hearing Chilean Expeditionary Force had sailed for the coast of Peru and we had instructions to keep them in sight.

The sea breeze sets in generally about 11. From the SW and falls towards sunset, remains calm and cool all night. The climate is a very fine one and not too hot. A certain amount of mist hangs about the land during the night and only clears up as the sun rises so it is always advisable if possible to make the anchorage by daylight.

---

33   Senor Serratea visits Rudolph's ship, HMS *Shannon*, 12 March 1880 at Ylo. On 30 May 1875, when serving on HMS *Cameleon*, Rudolph meets an old Oscottian, at Valparaiso Senor de Serratea: a proper gentlemen aged 70 with a charming wife and daughter.
34   Coquimbo, he visits again 9-18 August, 9-20 September 1880 and 16 March 1881.
35   British store ship anchored at Coquimbo, probably for the duration of hostilities. *Liffey*, which had been under sailing orders from 1 May at last sailed. She had been upon the point of sailing two or three times, but owing to the possibility of war, she was delayed each time. She was to relieve the old *Nereus* at Coquimbo as store ship, and for this purpose had her engines taken out and made the passage under sail. Frigate of 1856.
36   American steamer. Built Florida 1859, by order of the US Navy, sunk San Francisco, 1912.
37   Christopher R P Rodgers (1819-1892), Commander US Pacific Squadron 1877-1880, retired 1881. Flagship: US *Pensacola*.

HMS Turquoise.

There is a good place about one mile out, to land seamen and it is a fairly good cricket ground considering there is no grass.

During the winter there are snipe[38] to be had in the marshes. I got eleven one day but the season was over. There are numbers of fish in the small streams which are not tested whether they take a fly or not.

28 October   Took in 375 tons of coal and a long business it was, provisioned, but were hurried out again, just as we were settling down after our long cruise. Found La Serena[39] much the same as ever, little or no alteration in the place though the trees on the esplanade have grown a good deal in the last five years. Compania in many respects much improved, the gum tree wood being a delightful place and enormously grown; a few years ago one could look over any of them and now they are become really fine

---

38   Short-billed long legged bird.
39   365 miles north of Santiago; founded 1543, still a charming old world town. Population 72,000 (1977), 120,000 (2005).

HMS Thetis.

trees and afford delightful shade. The roses particularly are very fine; in fact, flowers tastefully arranged, with creepers everywhere and this is entirely artificial, for, owing to the absence of rain, nothing would grow above the level of the valley, but now it is all irrigated by steam power. The Lamberts, so well known for their hospitality to naval men, are at present in England, for their yacht, the *Wanderer* (700 tons) broke down in the Bay and had to return almost a wreck. The Blacks live in their house at present.

Having received a telegram from Captain Robinson[40] of the *Turquoise*[41], in answer to ours, weighed and proceeded north, in hopes of seeing some of the fun; made sail to a fresh SW breeze.

---

40   See entry for 22 November 1879.
41   British Corvette built 1876, 2162 tons, 1990 HP, sold 1892. Commissioned Sheerness, 13 September 1877.

30 October   Stopped off at Antofagasta[42] and communicated with mail steamer. This place, at the outbreak of the war, belonged to Bolivia, but was seized by the Chileans with very little loss, and made the base of operations during the present campaign. Learnt from the steamer, that the expedition had sailed, destination not known, supposed to be Arica. 7.50, proceeded in search of them.

31 October   The wind gradually decreasing as we get further north. Sighted the *Hugon*[43], French gun vessel ahead under sail, coming up astern under steam; we stopped, boarded her, and found her to be upon the same mission as ourselves. Reported having seen two steamers ahead, apparently on the look out, for they altered course, until apparently they had made us out, when they resumed their course.

1 November   Stopped off Iquique[44], communicated with Consul, no news. At 9.10 am proceeded north. 2.30 pm, looked into Pisagua[45] nothing going on, one French Barque at anchor.

2 November   7.40 am. Anchored in Arica[46] Roads in 11 fathoms; found here *Pelican*[47] sloop and Peruvian Monitor *Manco Capac*[48] and the small corvette *Pilcomayo*[49], both well surrounded by launches connected by hawsers. The former of these is level with water, steams about 4 knots and has one turret containing two 15 inch Rodman Guns[50] and protected by 8 single plates of 1 inch each bolted together about the equivalent of 5 inch armour. Prado[51] and Daza[52] the Commanders in Chief of the Peruvian and

---

42   1367 kms from Santiago. Population 225,000 (2005).
43   French Corvette built ?
44   Partly destroyed by earthquake in 1877, over 1,000 miles from Lima. Population 11,700 (1876), 65,000 (1977), 150,000 (2005).
45   Little town on narrow ledge at bottom of steep hills rising rapidly to over 1,000 feet.
46   See pages 121-126.
47   British sloop built 1877, sold 1901.
48   Peruvian Monitor (Floating Battery). Built USA 1864. Tons 1034. Scuttled Arica, Peru 7 June 1880.
49   Peruvian Corvette built 1873, tons 600, 108 HP. Captured by Chileans, 17 November 1879.
50   Invented by the American, Thomas Hefferson Rodman (1817-1871). Cast on hollow core whilst cooled internally by water.
51   Mariano Prado (1826-1901). Presidente of Peru 1876-1879.
52   Hilarion Daza (1840-1894). Presidente of Bolivia 1876-1880.

Bolivian armies were both here and the latter is President of the latter country.

11 am. Prado sent off a message to say the Chileans were bombarding Pisagua; weighed at once and steamed back to that place. Arica is the first place after leaving Coquimbo where one sees a blade of grass or a tree and there is little enough of either but the slightest indication of vegetation is at once seized upon the eye. Provisions, vegetables etc, are good in fact it is the only place where they grow; fruit can also be obtained but is expensive.

For hundreds of miles one passes up the coast seeing nothing but the same desert hills, sandy, of the same altitude and one place or other part resembling another so much so that, when one has seen one part, one has seen the whole. Few marks are there for the navigator but deep water extends close inshore, though it is always advisable to give the shore a berth of three miles as there are several rocks off the coast. About three miles from the town is the *Wateree*[53] an American man of war washed up by the tidal wave of '68 and left 500 yards inland.

The remains of the *America*[54] are to be seen about one mile out, the former ship has her back broken only, otherwise the shell is intact.

As soon as it was dark a large blaze on shore indicated the position of Pisagua[55], which was on fire, the stacks of coal blazing up and showing out clearly the shipping lying at anchor. About 9 o'clock felt a tremendous shock, though distant about five miles from the shore, so much so that many men who had turned in rushed on deck; the well was sounded but making no water, it was at first thought she had struck upon some wreck or by a torpedo but we found afterwards it was only an earthquake and a very severe one, the first I have ever felt when actually under weigh, we laid to under steam for the night.

---

53   American sidewheel gun vessel. Built Chester, USA 1864. Sold (wreck) 1868, 974 tons. Wrecked by earthquake and tidal wave, Arica, 15 August 1868. Landed by tidal wave 430 yards from high water mark.
54   Peruvian ship. Built 18? (wreck) 1869.
55   'The Battle of Pisagua' 2 November 1879. It was sketched by Rudolph and sent to his mother but has disappeared. In her diary for 24 February 1886, she states 'Mr Gleave, a large coke merchant from Leicester, called to see Gerard on business and had luncheon with us – he recognised all dear Rudolph's paintings, having been in Chile and Peru at that time of the year –   said the picture of the scaling up the hill and taking the fort took place exactly as represented at the battle of Pisagua.'.

3 November   At daylight, steamed in for the anchorage, picked up a billet near the *Turquoise* and *Thetis*[56] which ships had been present during the taking of the place. There were fifteen Chilean men of war and transports in the Bay; of the former were the *Cochrane*, *O'Higgins*, *Magallanes*[57] and *Covadonga*. These ships advanced and opened fire upon the town, the *Cochrane* on the right soon silenced the only fort (2 guns), set the town and coal on fire and, under cover of the guns of the ship and hidden by the smoke, the transports pushed forward with launches out ready, and disembarked a portion of the troops under a heavy fire from the shore; there were in all about 1,000 men defending the place, but their positions were badly selected; 300 were actually in the town itself, and were naturally driven out by the burning town; 500 were interspaced along the incline of the railway, but no rifle pits had been made, and the first line was stormed by a rush of the Atacama Regiment[58], and a company of the Chacabuco[59]. These men drove the Bolivians right up the face of the steep cliffs, the ships firing over their heads. The 2nd line, more than halfway up the face of the cliffs, was stubbornly resisted by about 100 men who, by the heaps of cartridges (empty), ought to have held the position for a long time and against great odds; as it was, they fired away as hard as they could, and inflicted comparatively little loss upon the Chileans. When their last cartridge was expended, they charged down with their bayonets and their bodies show, that in this place, they fought well.

The Chileans were so keen that their officers could not restrain them and they reached the top and planted the flag upon the summit; which, strange to say, they never attempted to hold. The Commandant bolted as soon as the firing began, otherwise, if well led, the Bolivians, no doubt, would have made a better defence. Before making the attack, the Chileans landed a force unobserved about three miles down the coast, and time was allowed for them to march round and take the Bolivians in flank, but the charge of the Atacama Regiment spoilt this, for the remnant of the defenders had bolted before their arrival, otherwise the whole force would have been captured. The Chileans

---

56 British Corvette, built 1871, 1870 tons, 2275 HP, sold 1887. Commissioned Devonport 13 May 1879.
57 Chilean Warship. 772 tons, 260 HP.
58 Chilean Regiment named after Northern Desert.
59 Chilean Regiment named after Chilean City.

lost about 80 killed and 200 wounded; the Bolivian loss being more than double that number. The killed were laying all over the face of the cliff. In batches of fives and sixes, the Chilean authorities were very slack in having the bodies buried but showed a little more energy after our captain declared the sight to be revolting. All day the Chileans were engaged disembarking their troops, guns and cavalry and I must say the whole thing was conducted in capital style; the cavalry only 1,000 strong I believe were in capital condition and well cared for and groomed, armed with Winchester carbines[60]. The infantry with the Comblain rifle[61], and all remarkably well shod; their general appearance was very good and soldierlike, particular attention being paid to the foreign officers, the men standing to attention and saluting. They landed 35 Krupp Guns[62] and 15 other guns and Gatling[63] 2 or 3 of the latter.

Forage there was in abundance, and the Commissariat seemed to work well, but the want of water completely tied their hands and water had to be condensed by the ship, and it was four days before the condensors on shore were in working order.

Strangely enough, the Bolivians never destroyed the railway, and actually left a couple of trains in perfect working order, which naturally assisted the Chileans enormously with the transit of provisions, munitions etc. The Bolivians had a camp upon the top of the hill (height 1,080 feet instead of 2,600 from Chilean accounts) which was deserted, and turned into account at once by their enemies. The Chacabucos held the advanced posts about six miles across the plain, and in a gorge overlooking the next plain. For the whole country is a succession of these with ranges of hills, varying from 1,000 to 2,500 feet high, deep loose sand everywhere.

The only passes were never held by the Bolivians but simply occupied by their adversaries. Two days after, the cavalry, with fifteen guns, advanced one night upon Agua Santa, which they took without much resistance, captured more engines, number of trucks and the chief thing – the wells. This place, was of course, of vital importance

---

60   The Winchester (repeating) Arm Co formed 1866. Oliver F. Winchester, Walter Hunt, Lewis Jennings and Horace Smith are all serious contenders as possible inventors of the underlever principle.
61   As later applied to the Winchester rifle.
62   First made under the supervision of Alfred Krupp (1812-1887) in Essen, Germany.
63   Invented by the American, Richard J Gatling (1818-1903): constant rifle fire from 8/10 barrels revolving on an axis.

to them, as they were no longer tied down to rationing of their water, or having it sent along the line by rail. The troops were more than thirty hours without water, and the unfortunate wounded Bolivians in the camp were not better off; several officers took wine with them, up the line, and it did one good to see the poor fellows' thankful faces as they drank it. Not a single one of them muttered a groan, though very severely wounded, and some mortally. General Escala[64] was in command of the Chileans, and highly spoken of and much liked by the soldiers.

The landing at Pisagua was undertaken, the force landed being 9,960 men, which force was reinforced later by 3,500 men from Antofagasta and Reserves from Valparaiso with the intention of taking Iquique; the Fleet joined by the *Huascar* making the attack by sea.

4 November   On the 4th the *Turquoise* and *Pelican* were sent down to Iquique.

10 November   We remained until 10th when we left for that place. Pisagua was, at best, always a miserable place, but was utterly destroyed; the only building remaining being the British Consulate.

Started about midnight and arrived at 10.30 am and anchored in 15 fathoms. Found here *Turquoise*, US Corvette *Alaska*[65] and *Hugon*, French gun vessel. The town was almost deserted, the people expecting to be bombarded at any time. There were a fair number of vessels laying off the place, and numbers of launches showing their respective colours, and in these, many of the foreigners lived; those who remained on shore had mostly buried their goods, and constructed a bomb-proof dwelling, where in case of need, they might burrow. Two forts comprise the defence of the place; one facing north, the other the south and westward, one gun being able to bear to the north over the town. One 300 pounder and one 150 pounder Parrot guns[66] in each battery, a dismounted gun (recovered from the *Independencia*[67] Ironclad, which vessel was decoyed on to the rocks,

---

64   Chilean; General Erasmo Escala (1826-1884).
65   American Corvette, built Boston USA 1868, 2400 tons. Sold 1883.
66   Invented by the American, Robert Parrot.
67   Peruvian Ironclad, built Thames 1865, 2004 tons, 550 HP. Sunk Iquique, Peru 21 May 1879. Commandante Aurelio Garcia y Garcia (see page 170).

and lost whilst chasing the little *Covadonga* and trying to ram her) of about 9 tons but they had forgotten to get any projectiles for it, so there it lay; but their (the Peruvian) motto in everything seems to be *Manana*; but no wonder they are dispirited, for the Chileans have complete command of the sea and can land anywhere they choose.

Strange that perhaps the fate of the country should depend upon the loss of a single ship, but these countries do not run to many ships though, if Peruvian accounts are to be credited, soon will the *Manana, Mas Tarde* and *Poco Tempo* make their appearance, but where they are coming from, or what class of ships they are, still remains a state secret. These names were found for them by some wit in Lima, and are, no doubt, very appropriate ones.

The Commandant of Iquique, for ten days after our arrival, continued making preparations for the reception of the Chileans when they should arrive before the place, organising the National Guard in all about 1,200 strong, but most of them of very poor quality. The officers in charge of the forts seemed to have little idea of distance or the range of their guns, and not a single beacon was laid down as a guide to them.

15 November   On the 15th, there was great excitement on shore for the *Cochrane* and *Covadonga* were made out steering straight for the town. The former sent a boat in and communicated with the authorities, and informed them that ten days would be allowed for the merchant ships to clear out, and would not fire at the place at all unless fired upon, and would also keep outside so as to give them no unreasonable cause of offence.

22 November   On the 22nd, orders were received at Iquique from General Buendia[68] ordering the immediate evacuation of the town, the dismantling of the forts, and the troops to make the best of their way to Tarapaca[69] to join the troops already assembled there. The next day the troops were seen streaming over the hill, the consuls taking charge of the town until the Chileans entered, which they did next day, the *Cochrane* having dispatched the *Covadonga* with the news to Pisagua and troops were immediately sent to take possession, and all this without a shot having been fired.

---

68   Peruvian; General Juan Buendia (1816-1895).
69   Inland city from Iquique.

On the 12th, the captain of the *Turquoise*[70] invalided and Commander McKechnie[71] went as acting captain of her, Holbech[72] becoming Acting Commander and Oliver[73] acting Lieutenant. We made one wonderful haul of fish but they were of poor quality, a sort of pilchard. The harbour simply teemed with fish of this sort but, off the island, rock cod were obtained by means of torpedoes.

Iquique is the place the Chileans had landed the force at Pisagua, to take wishing to push their base of operations further on, Antofagasta being too far away, but there is little doubt that it might haven been carried by a *coup de main*.

The *Pelican* was sent off to Callao[74], to give the news to the admiral[75]. The wire to the northward having been cut by the blockading squadron, one of their first acts after taking the place, was to connect the Southern wire with Antofagasta. The *Pelican's* boiler, or rather one of them, blew up off Callao through the negligence of the Officer of the Watch who let the water down; three men were unfortunately killed and several injured. The *Turquoise* was ordered off the same day to Arica, the consul having telegraphed for a ship. The *Decies*[76] French Corvette relieved the *Hugon* who sailed for the south homeward bound and soon the *Hussard*[77] and *Chasseur*[78] made their appearance (sloops with an enormous ram bow to support the guns forward more than for offensive purposes). These two vessels are exceedingly useful, most economical steamers, have a maximum speed of 13.5 knots and sail very well for their size and have made 11 under these conditions. Heavily armed, but guns totally unprotected; four 12 centimetre guns mounted upon a turntable amidships the bulwarks being lowered out of the way of the fire. She (*Hussard*) also has Hotchkiss gun[79] and most destructive one it is (revolving and six barrels). By an ingenious contrivance, the cartridges used for

70   See entry for 28 October 1879 as to Captain Robinson of the *Turquoise*.
71   Alexander McKechnie, temporary captain of HMS *Turquoise* 12 November 1879-20 February 1880. Appointed 17 July 1877, HMS *Shannon*.
72   Lt Edward A Holbech (1846-1915). Appointed 7 November 1877, HMS *Shannon*.
73   Lt Oliver. Promoted to HMS *Pelican*, February 1880.
74   Main port of Peru, 10 miles from Lima. Population 33,500 (1876); 400,000 (1977); 600,000 (2005).
75   Rear Admiral Frederick Stirling (1829-1886). Commander British Pacific Squadron 1879-1881. Appointed 21 July 1879, Flagship HMS *Triumph* (1873).
76   French Corvette, built 18?
77   French sloop, built 18?
78   French sloop, built 1878.
79   Invented by the American, Benjamin B Hotchkiss (1826-1885). Fed by continuous metallic strip and cooled due to thick barrel.

drill purposes form perfect little rifled gun of itself, and an ordinary fusil; gras cartridge, fitting into the breach, is fired by this method instead of using one of the expensive shell cartridges. These vessels stow 150 tons of coal and the *Hussard,* we were told, can steam seventy-five days at the rate of 6 knots and 10 at rate 13.5. The former, an expenditure of two tons of coal a day. The *Chasseur* has different engines and is not so economical though her speed is the same.

6 December   We remained at Iquique until the 6th, when we left for Arica about 9 pm. We passed Pisagua and the *Blanco Encalada* turned her electric light upon us, and a small gun boat came out, fired a gun, thinking possibly we were the *Manana* on our way north, but as we burnt a blue light, she unnecessarily delayed us. However the captain came on board and apologised and we proceeded next day.

7 December   Sighted the *Cochrane, Covadonga* and armed transport off Arica blockading; stopped and communicated with the former ship and gave them some vegetables for which they were very thankful.

Arica
Found here the *Alaska* (US Corvette), *Turquoise* and *Gannet, Decies* French Corvette. The town is protected by the battery of ten parrot guns (150 pounder) on the top of El Morro[80], but mounted so close to the precipitous edge, that they run grave dangers of being dismounted by a well regulated fire at the summit of this sold cliff, for so it is. There are three other batteries, sandworks containing two guns each (150 pounder Parrot) and cased with clods of turf.

The Peruvians refused to allow us to see any of the works inside, so great is their dislike of us. But it is the same everywhere on the Peruvian coast, and the *Huascar* and *Shah* affair[81] is the cause. We have not added laurels to the English Naval history by this

80   Arica, Natural Mountain.
81   *Huascar,* 6 May 1877, rebelled and Peruvian Government asked all ships to capture *Huascar.* But Admiral Horsey ordered *Shah* (1873) and *Amethyst* (1873) to chase *Huascar.* Pierola joined rebels on *Huascar* and Captain Juan Moore commanded *Independencia* which then pursued *Huascar.* Caught the *Huascar,* 30 May, and its rebels were sent back to Callao and were amnestied by Prado.

business, though in the List of Meritorious acts etc, in the Navy List everyone who was present in the action is mentioned as though it had been a glorious victory. We had several games of cricket; played *Shannon* versus other ships; in the first match we were beaten but in the 'return' won in one innings. Officers only playing.

13 December   We sighted cavalry and infantry, about 2,000 in all coming in; the remnants from Tarapaca, this reinforcement augments the force to something like 8,000 men or more. They do not compare with the Chilean troops in appearance, discipline or equipment, and are nearly all full bloodied Indians, Carne Para El Poncho, as they are called. Well led, could be invaluable, for they thoroughly enjoy fighting, and are fully assured they can beat the Chileans on shore at least.

15 December   Left Arica for Callao. Having received orders by the *Thetis* instead of going south as we had intended, that very day.

19 December   Slight fog in the morning, no sights though we were close to the land but at noon got the latitude and soon the fog cleared though the air was full of moisture and freshened to quite a strong breeze when off San Lorenzo. 3.20 pm anchored in Callao Bay with Callao Point S8°24'W, Mole Light House N83°24'W.

Callao

Found here *Triumph*[82] (Rear Admiral Stirling), *Pelican*, *Pensacola* US frigate bearing flag of Rear Admiral Rogers, *Victorieuse*[83] French Ironclad flag of Contre Amiral du Petit Thouars[84], *Hussard,* French Gun vessel, Italian frigate *Garibaldi*. As soon as we arrived we heard that the President, Prado[85], had sailed that very evening for Europe via

---

82   British Ironclad, built 1870, 6640 tons, 4892 HP, retired 1904, Flagship Rear Admiral F Stirling. Commissioned Portsmouth, 1 May 1878.
83   French Ironclad, built 18? Flagship Contre Admiral B du Petit Thouars.
84   Contre Amiral Bergasse du Petit Thouars (1832-1890) Commander French, Pacific Squadron 1878-1881 (see page 72).
85   Mariano Prado (1826-1901). President 1865-1868, 1876-1879. Mariano Prado was authorised and encouraged by the Peruvian Congress and Cabinet to travel swiftly to Europe to obtain further military supplies. He left Lima on 18 December 1879 and reached New York – via Panama – on 6 January 1880. He was astounded to discover that, in his absence, he had been deposed and was therefore no longer empowered to purchase armaments in Europe. Rudolph's information appear to have been gleaned from rumours and the majority of historians have not regarded Prado's action as anything but patriotic.

Almirante Labrano (1834-1896).   *Amiral Bergasse du Petit Thouars (1832-1890).*

Panama but had over £100,000 with him, perhaps to invest in the *Manana*? La Puerta[86] took his place and said to be a very good man.

21 December   Revolution in Lima[87]. Pierola[88] acknowledged as President, it came about in this way. Immediately Prado sailed, people began talking about Pierola as the most competent man to succeed him and a crowd gathered in the Grand Plazza[89] and armed. La Cotera[90] (Minister of War), hearing cries of 'Viva el Pierola', sent to Aquerda[91] to bring

86   Peruvian; General Luis la Puerta (1811-1896). President 1879-?
87   Capital of Peru, population 120,000 (1866), 3^1/$_2$ million (1977), c8,000,000 (2005).
88   Peruvian; General Nicolas de Pierola (1839-1913). President 1879-1881.
89   Properly 'Plaza de Armas' which in Spain would be called 'Plazza Mayor'.
90   Peruvian; General Manuel de la Cotera, Minister of War 18?.-18?
91   Peruvian; Major Pablo Arguedas.

Lima Cathedral.

his regiment to the town to fire upon and dismiss the people assembled. This man replied, he had equipped his regiment 650 strong himself without any aids from the Government and on purpose to fight the Chilenos but not to fire upon his own people and refused, he was then ordered to surrender himself to La Cotera and give up his arms and disband his men. He replied, 'My body they might take and my men's arms if they can take them'.

Two battalions were then ordered out to disarm them, and field pieces brought up;

Entrance to the Camber, Callao, Peru.

The Ica Regiment[92] taking up position on the top of the barracks near the Plaza el Bolivar[93]. At 6pm the firing began, one of the field pieces bursting and killing several men. Pierola at this time was unable to show himself, for the barracks of the troops he depended upon were commanded by the Santa Catalina Fort[94], but at 7.30 pm his regiments emerged to the attack upon the palace and to the relief of the Ica regiment. The firing now was simply tremendous, for an hour without intermission one unceasing roll of musketry, broken by the sound of the field pieces. A regiment, or portion of one of the cavalry, attacks the troops in the square and are driven pell mell down one street

---

92 Peruvian Regiment named after Southern City.
93 Formerly called 'Plazza de la Inquisition' since the Inquisition had its nefarious HQ there since 1570.
94 Built 1806.

(to the *Hotel de France et d'Angleterre*[95]) more than 200 strong with numbers of horses riderless, volleys rattle after them but flying high. Then come seven more, three horses riderless, and last, the officer in charge as cool as possible, holding his horse well in hand, and without moving a muscle, an exceedingly fine looking fellow.

The palace[96] is at length stormed, or rather the troops within turned round, where once it was freed and declared for Pierola. La Cotera rode about in the Plazza encouraging his men, and got a bullet through his kepi, and turned round and bound in the direction the bullet had come from. The sympathies of the crowd were with the new President, but they soon cleared the streets when the cavalry charged. About 8.40 the firing ceased and we emerged; found about fifty dead bodies, six horses lying on the

95   Hotel in centre of Lima.
96   Presidential Palace, on site of Pizzaro's Palace. Much altered. New one finished 1938.

cathedral[97] steps and inside two officers and ghastly they looked all killed by bullet wound. Most of the dead were carried off by their friends as soon as they fell – but the Plaza Bolivar was the scene of the hardest fighting; now it is acknowledged that 280 were killed, and about three times or more than that number wounded. Aquerda was wounded, but his brave regiment did not lose many, though they inflicted heavy losses upon their opponents. The troops, poor fellows, were led out not knowing what the fighting was about and were told to take places held by their own men. Obedient to the death, these poor fellows did their duty, for what could they do but obey their official orders, and then they fell. One poor fellow fell mortally wounded and exclaimed, *'Muerte por mi hermano yo no quiero si este pais l'enemigo'* showing how intensely they feel fighting internally with the enemy at their gates so to speak. The present Government are doing their utmost to hush the whole affair up 'lest their enemies, the Chileans, take courage by their internal disorders' but the news will leak soon enough.

Pierola marched down at 4 am to Lima with a few regiments and there was a meeting of the colonels of the regiments to decide what was to be done; it was ultimately decided to favour his election which Callao did with acclamation. The greater number of troops at Lima were merely lookers on, and supposed to support La Cotera but before the next day they all agreed to elect Pierola instead of fighting it out and this man seems to be acknowledged as the most capable man, though utterly unscrupulous.

He has always been an agitator; in '71 he first made himself prominent there in the

---

97 Cathedral, first built by Francisco Pizarro in 1535 and rebuilt 1765 after the earthquake of 1746.

98 In 1871, General Tomas Gutierrez, Peruvian, Minister of War, committed treason against President Balta; he led an uprising, captured the President and had him shot. Rudolph describes this in a letter (from Panama, 4 August 1872) to his mother which is quoted in his Memoir p.52/3: 'The Secretary of War at Lima, having got all the soldiers at his side, suddenly threw the Governor, or – I should say – President, into prison, and then set up for himself and proclaimed martial law, as will be imagined. The people would not stand this, and the forts were stormed by them, and the Secretary slaughtered. Three brothers, Guitanis by name, three of the greatest scoundrels (then) alive, set up for themselves, and the eldest, a Colonel Toho, commanding the forces of Lima, was shot dead as he arrived at the station. His next brother then took charge, and determined on revenge; he found entrance to the President's prison, and stabbed and mutilated him horribly, he himself escaping, but just as he was getting into the train, he was dragged out and stabbed by all those around. The last brother, seeing all chance of success hopeless, attempted to hide till everything was quiet; he hid in a large apothecary's shop, and there he was found by the populace, who despatched him with their daggers, and the bodies of the three were by public order hanged in the principal plaza and then buried. Pablo is the new President, and he only just escaped the Guitanis by getting on board one of the men-of-war. Everything is now quiet again, but several people who have nothing to do with the politics of the country were shot, some think to pay off old scores.'

Guttieres[98] affair and now; but there is little doubt that he will remain President until either he has made his pile or else until assassinated by some scoundrel. The exchange on gold since his accession to power is at $68 instead of $92 but how long it will rise it is hard to say probably until the Chilean fleet heave in sight when it will fall to $100 perhaps. The country seems to be tottering upon national bankruptcy and there is not a single statesman who has the moral courage to say they have had the worst of it and make terms upon the best terms they may; for they have no ships and, upon any portion of their coast, an enemy can land. The Bolivians who did all the first fighting seem inclined to leave them and come to terms when no doubt they will receive Tacna[99] (Province) with Arica for a sea port and they themselves take the whole coast as far as Iquique or Pisagua. The former is a great place for the export of nitrate of soda and also the silver mines when developed will produce large quantities of ore. All the English there seem to look forward to a more settled Government and to the abolition of bribery.

The Exhibition Gardens[100] and buildings are very nice; the former is always a shady retreat from the heat of the sun, but it is no longer tended with the same care it was; everywhere the same neglect and deserted almost entirely. Since the loss of the *Huascar* the nation has gone into mourning; no parties or gaiety of any sort, no dances for the populace would break anyone's windows who permitted it. The botanical gardens are nice but also neglected and open 2 to 7. Not so shady as the other however.

The principal feature of Lima is of course the cathedral and churches; the first of these has been spoilt by the restoration. It had a venerable look about it which has been quite lost in the restoration. It is however a fine building. The San Francisco[101] and Mercedes[102] are however fine churches. The San Augustin[103] has a fine façade but is quite spoilt inside by the trumpery ornamentation; this is the fault to be found everywhere unfortunately. But no doubt it suits the people who think, or would think our churches cold. The organs are good and the services better done than when I was here a few years ago.

---

99   The city had a population of 7,800 (1876) but 175,000 (2005).
100 Opened 1868 for the International Exhibition; the main Palace is now the Museum of Art.
101 Baroque Church; begun 1535 and finished 1674.
102 Baroque Church; begun 1534. First Mass in Lima said on this spot.
103 Baroque Church; begun 1554.

22 December   The *Union* Peruvian Corvette made her appearance, contradicting by her presence the rumour that she had been captured by the *Blanco Encalada*.

24 December   The midnight service on Christmas Eve was well done in the Mercedes but not too well attended. The best hotel in Lima is that of *France et d'Angleterre*, very reasonable and comfortable. Horses were to be hired at $20 a day! This seems astounding but for the time the Sol is only worth about a shilling.

The trip by train to the top of the Andes viz; to Chicla[104] (12,200 feet) is well worth seeing I believe but it requires 3 or 4 days leave, so it is a trip to look forward to should we not be sent out of it.

25 December   HMS *Triumph* arrived having heard by telegram of the Revolution in Lima; she however arrived too late to see anything. She was laying off Mollendo[105] at the time on her way South.

Christmas Day passed off very quietly on board but the lower deck was not decorated or anything to show what the festival was. Both watches were given general leave and most of them found their way up to Lima and seem to enjoy the gardens etc. One batch of these, amused us rather by going and dining at the best hotel where they had to pay at least $7 or 8 for their dinner, but expense to them was nothing and they seemed bent upon enjoying themselves.

28 December   8 am. HMS *Osprey*[106] arrived and anchored. She did not distinguish herself in the way she anchored. She is only here for a short time when she leaves for Pitcairn Island[107] and the Islands[108] and is expected back in about six months.

---

104   Town at altitude of 3734 metres (12,250 feet) and 71 miles East of Lima.
105   Until recently, main port for Arequipa. Population 1,400 (1866), 14,250 (1977), 30,000 (2005).
106   British sloop, built 1876 and sold 1890 – Captain: Commander Hon Holmes A'Court.
107   Small and volcanic, midway between New Zealand and Panama; descendants of mutineers of HMS *Bounty*. Rudolph visited mid-1873 and sketched these.
108   Pacific Islands which Rudolph visited extensively mid-1873.

1880

few words may here be said of the remnants of the Peruvian Navy which consists of the *Union* Corvette carrying 11 x 70 pr ML guns of French pattern and able to steam, 14 knots but has the grave danger of having its boilers burst by a shell entering the tops of them, being three feet above the water line. A pretty vessel and with very fine lines, French built. *Atahualpa*[1] an old monitor (American) protected by ten inch laminated iron on water line and turret with a flying deck. Mounts 2 x 500 pr Rodman guns; but engines worn out and not able to steam more than 4.5 knots; still being level with the water might be capable of inflicting damage with small prospect of being herself hit. The *Rimac*[2], *Chalaco*[3] and *Oroya*[4] Transports, armed transports, the former was captured by the *Huascar* from the Chileans in the early part of the war; so pleased were the Peruvians of their capture, that the Sol notes of last issue were stamped with her representation. The *Manco Capac* sister vessel to the *Atahualpa* and incapable of steaming more than 2.5 or 3 knots and down at Arica. During the month of January, the Callao 'painter'[5] is particularly offensive, the water becomes a deep brown colour and emits a most sickly stench and discolours paintwork chiefly of boats; an hour or so in the water is sufficiently long to utterly ruin the paintwork of any boat. The 'painter' lasts generally for three or four days but near the new Mole it is always more or less bad.

30 December/1 January 1880 The Admiral's Inspection; he did not seem fascinated by the ship's general appearance as our late Com in Chief and left the ship without saying

---

1   Peruvian Monitor (Floating battery). Built USA 1864. 1034 tons 350 HP. Sunk Iquique, Peru, 21 May 1879.
2   Peruvian Transport. Captured from Chileans 23 July 1879. Scuttled 1881.
3   Peruvian Transport (steamer), 999 tons. Scuttled 1881.
4   Peruvian Transport.
5   Strange local water condition.

a word; he made us lay out and stream anchor and weigh it again, it was rather awkward doing so on account of the slight chop of a sea and weight of the anchor (30 cwt).

8 January   HMS *Turquoise* arrived from the south.

10 January   HMS *Osprey* sailed.

21 January   *La Victorieuse* sailed for Valparaiso. The regatta took place today at least a part of it *viz*: the Sailing Races; our first cutter was the only boat who took a 1st prize belonging to the ship, our Pinnace in spite of the supreme efforts of Oliver, failed to win, came in one of the last. The Admiral's Race for £5 was a very pally race, a good fresh breeze blowing, every sail was filled. The boats starting according to their class and with a time allowance. The launches and pinnaces looked very pretty at the start with their cloud of sail all set, in a moment gaff topsails and spinnakers were set and the boats went flying down to the first buoy; hauled their wind in spinnakers and topsails, too much wind in them and up to the second and there a dead heat back; our Pinnace coming in nowhere. The *Shannon* entertained a great number of people on board, it having been arranged with the *Triumph* that this ship should do the honours today, the *Triumph* the following day. Our band played very well and the dancing appeared to be more enjoyed even than the races. The most exciting part of a race failed to withdraw some of our fair visitors from the still more seductive waltz and even the gun fired to announce the victory failed to withdraw them to witness the finish. The dancing was kept up until dark and many were the regrets that all was over for the day. Our first cutter managed to get the cutters prize. The next day saw the pulling races. The *Shannon* coming well to the fore for she succeeded in getting five or six prizes. The Stokers Race a particularly good one and won by ours in the 4th cutter; for us (officers) the exciting race was the Officers Race in whalers. The *Turquoise's* coming in an easy first, our boat and the *Triumph's* fouling at the first and second buoys; the three boats went down to the first buoy almost a dead heat. The prize was a cup given by Messrs Grace of Callao[6] and we made up our minds that at least the flagships should not win it.

---

6   Large American firm.

For some time previous we, Messrs Job[7] (stroker), de Lisle[8], Stileman[9], Walrond[10] Martin[11], de Robeck[12] (coxswain) had been practising three times a day, but our whaler was never considered a good boat and came in nowhere in the Blue Jacket whaler race. We tried very hard to get the *Pelican's* whaler but the captain objected and so did the Committee, so we had to pull in our own.

The Punt Races were amusing; the usual capsizes much to the amusement of the visitors. The *Shannon's* happened to be the only one that pulled round the course or received the prize.

The *Triumph* was crowded with visitors but her officers were very much disgusted at not winning the Officers Race.

Our 4th cutter in the pulling races particularly distinguished herself winning two 1st prizes.

24 January   The *Triumph* sailed for the still north leaving us senior officers down south.

Note of weather for January

The weather was very fine on the whole, though fogs were frequent for a short time in the early morning, but generally lifted as the sun came out, wind SE varying from a force of 1 to 3.4, although January is one of the hottest months in the year, the average maximum was only 71° in the shade. In the sun however, it was occasionally very hot.

2 February   Departed this life, Charles Taylor[13] (Caulkers Mate).

---

7   Thomas, Job, boatswain. Appointed, 17 July 1877, HMS *Shannon.*
8   Rudolph M P de Lisle (1853-1885). Appointed 30 November 1878, HMS *Shannon.*
9   Harry H Stileman, Acting Sub-Lieut. Appointed 17 March 1880 HMS *Shannon.*
10 Arthur M H Walrond, Midshipman. Appointed 28 January 1878 HMS *Shannon.*
11 Edward Martin, Sub-Lieut. Appointed HMS *Shannon.*
12 John M de Robeck, Midshipman. Appointed 27 July 1878 HMS *Shannon.*
13 Charles Taylor (Cankers Mate). The British Cemetery, Lima states he died 1 Feb 1880.

3 February   Short funeral party ashore to inter the remains of the late Charles Taylor in the cemetery at Bella Vista.[14]

7 February   Sailed HMS *Pelican*.

11 February   US Flagship *Pensacola* we were all very sorry when she left for she had a very nice lot of fellows on board and the two ships were very friendly. We had a game of baseball with them during their stay and we (*Shannon* and Flag[15]) got thoroughly beaten, but then it was the first time we had played. We played them twice at cricket and beat them very easily, in one innings both times. They had a very good band on board and gave a very nice dance just before they left; Admiral Rodgers an exceedingly courteous man and liked by everyone.

20 February   Captain Medlycott[16] joined the *Turquoise* and Commander McKechnie[17] returned to the ship having been away as Acting Captain for four months.

21 February   Italian frigate *Garibaldi* sailed.

25 February   Sailed HMS *Turquoise* for Coquimbo.

26 February   The Mail steamer to the north sailed having on board Henry Ponsonby[18] (Lieutenant) and Oliver[19] (Lieutenant) on promotion and appointed to the *Pelican*. There is no doubt the ship has suffered a great loss by losing these two officers, for two more genial shipmates could not be found; they were pulled on board by a boats crew of officers who cheered them lustily; as the moment of parting arrived, our band played

---

14   Near Callao; now called Cementerio Baquedano.
15   HMS *Triumph*, Flagship of Rear Admiral Stirling (1829-1886).
16   Capt Mervyn Medlycott. Actually nominated 10 December 1879 to HMS *Turquoise*.
17   Alexander G McKechnie. Acting Captain HMS *Turquoise*, 12 November 1879 – 20 February 1880, from HMS *Shannon*.
18   Lt Henry Ponsonby (HP) invalided February 1880, HMS *Shannon*.
19   Acting Lieut in HMS *Turquoise*, 12 November 1879 – 26 February 1880. From HMS *Shannon*.

*Chilean Armour-plated Turret ship Huascar after her foremast was
taken out by a shell at the bombardment of Arica.*

suitable music and wound up with a waltz knowing how it would cheer up the Old Man
to hear the same old tune so oft repeated. A signal followed the steamer as she sped
away northward 'wishing them speedy voyage and goodbye' to which she replied
'thank you'. HP was one of those men who are always cheerful under all circumstances,
full of anecdotes and a wonderful facility in relating them; no one could remain in his
society for any length of time without acquiring a certain amount of his warmth.

He was a keen sportsman, a good shot and rider and considerably augmented our
list of game at Bashika[20] and Smyrna[21].

---

20   Rudolph was there first, on HMS *Pallas*, April-July 1876 and shot during the four months 1000 head (including 721 snipe)
and again on HMS *Shannon*, January 1879 and shot snipe, woodcocks, hares '….and for the next six weeks they were cruising
about in the Mediterranean, between Vourlah Bay, Cyprus, Malta, Sicily, and Naples.'
21   Rudolph was there, on HMS *Pallas* July 1876 and again on HMS *Shannon* March 1879 and shot nearby (at Kyas and
Trianda); Rudolph sketched the city in 1876 (see watercolour, page 36).

Landing of the Chilean Army at Ylo before the battle of Tacna. Angamos (Lynch), Abtao, Pilcomayo, Huascar, Janaqueo (Thorneycroft), Guacolda, Blanco Encalada (R. Ad. Riveros).

With a 'Matabeesh' he could hold his own with any of his shipmates and as an actor or, rather, Tragedian – first class. It was he who first discovered the theatrical talent up to this time latent in the ship, and it was he who succeeded in developing it to its present state; this loss to the 'officer's theatrical party' is irreparable and they will ever remember him in his last appearance in the 'Belle of the Barley Mow' when he carried the house by storm. His greatest principle of 'Give and Take' he developed to the utmost, though it must be confessed that at times the 'Give' seemed to be swallowed up

84

in the 'Take' and the latter aforesaid more deeply grafted in him than the former. He contrived however to persuade the other watch keepers how necessary it was that the two should be equal and they to show their love of this great Principle drew up a memorandum which after some opposition on his part, at length received his signature and theirs which virtually made the 'Give equal to the Take!' He was invalided and left regretted by all.

6 March   HMS *Gannet* arrived from Arica; brought news of the action fought between the *Huascar* and *Manco Capac*. It appears the *Magallanes* (Chilean) keeping in too close to the Morro was fired upon, she returned the fire, the *Huascar* joining in. Capt

Sanchez Lagomarsino[22] seeing the *Huascar* close in, determined to try the effect of his smooth bores at close range so weighed and steered out towards the *Huascar*, the *Manco* going 2.5 knots. The *Huascar* tried to ram but somehow passed just ahead of her adversary and received the contents of the 500 pounder; Capt Thompson[23], 1 mid and 13 men were killed and 13 wounded. The *Huascar* now became apparently demoralised and, after a shot or so, made use of her speed 10 or 11 knots to clear out of range, the *Manco* having no speed did not follow but returned to her anchorage under the Morro.

8 March   2pm. Weighed and proceeded to sea.

9/10 March   Exercised at General Quarters firing shot and shell at a target.

11 March   6pm. Passed by Mollendo, observed the place to be on fire, saw two Chilean vessels looming through the smoke.

12 March   7 am. Anchored off Ylo[24] in 17 fathoms. Anchorage bearings, Outer Rock off Ylo R. N16°E. Railway Chimney S40°E.

Ylo

Found here Chilean vessels *Abtao*[25] and *Angamos*[26] and nine transports. The Chileans had landed altogether 16,000 men, but two days previously 2,000 had been sent to Mollendo, and had destroyed the place; they were to return to Ylo on the 14th. 4,000 had been pushed to the front and had occupied Moquegua[27]. The remainder go to the front almost immediately. 35 Krupp field guns had been landed and a few Brass Guns

---

22   Peruvian; Captain Jose Sanchez Lago Marsino of *Manco Capac*.
23   Chilean; Captain Manuel Thompson (? -1880) *Huascar* 1880.
24   Port City for Moquegua.
25   Chilean Transport (corvette), 1051 tons 300 HP.
26   Chilean steamer. Commanded by Patrick Lynch (1824-1886).
27   Peruvian city 150 miles from Arequipa at 4,000 ft. Population 3,600 (1876), 10,000 (1977), 110,000 (2005).

M.L. The Chileans have a very great advantage over the Peruvians both in artillery and cavalry; the Chilean horses seemed in capital condition and were in first rate spirits. Serratea[28] came on board with another Chileno and lunched with me. At 5pm we sailed for Arica. Montgomerie[29] went out to the river to see if he could get any duck; he failed to see any, shot a couple of pigeons.

13 March Daylight arrived: Chilean Blockading Squadron off Arica (*Huascar*, *Magallanes* and *Matias Cousino*) 10.30 anchored near the *Wateree*[30] observing all the neutral ships had cleared out of the line of fire; we were consequently about two miles from the town. The neutrals consisted of the *Hansa*[31], *Garibaldi* and *Hussard*. The *Manco Capac* as usual at anchorage under the Morro. In the afternoon some of us landed to see the effect of the *Angamos*'s bombardment; the results were small and of no moment though several buildings bore witness of their being victims to her fire. Had the place been inflammable, there is no doubt it would have been destroyed, but made as it is of some dried bricks and mud it cannot ignite.

On the 29 February, she arrived and opened fire; the inhabitants cleared out of the town to Tacna and the troops marched out and encamped under cover of a sand hill; for six consecutive days she kept up the bombardment firing from 12 to 15 shots a day and firing at a range of 8,000 yards with her now famous Armstrong gun [a few words *en passant* about it will not be amiss. It is an improved Armstrong[32] with a large powder chamber capable of receiving 90 lbs of powder in two bags; the system of loading as the French, the rifling his own, the projectiles 180 lbs, weight of gun $11\frac{1}{2}$ tons, 8 inch calibre, and length 18ft 4 ins. A great length certainly but the gun is capable of enormous range owing to this and its capacity for firing such a large battering charge; our 18 ton guns, the Battering charge is only 70 and here with a $11\frac{1}{2}$ ton gun, 90 lbs is used].

The forts were unable to send their shot more than halfway so she had all the fire

---

28 Rudolph knew the Serratea family from previous visits and saw them on 20 October 1879 at Valparaiso. (see page 60)
29 Lt Robert A J Montgomerie. Appointed 20 July 1879, HMS *Shannon*.
30 See page 64, note 53.
31 German Corvette built 1872. 4404 tons. Retired 1888.
32 Improved Armstrong gun (see page 59).

on her side. Note: The projectiles used by Armstrong guns have no studs but a gas check. The gun is mounted on a turntable amidships and fires from both sides but only abeam or at least not more than 15° before and abaft. This, of course, is a great disadvantage, for the ship would have to turn if running from an Ironclad to fire her gun; but the arming of the *Angamos* shows what can be done with a vessel of great speed with a proper gun. When it was thought we were going to war with Russia, steamers (merchants) were to be fitted-out to protect our commerce and armed with 2 x 64 Pounders; much better to have them armed with bows and arrows; on this point we have learnt a wrinkle from the Chileans or rather from Sir W. Armstrong.

13 March   *Garibaldi* sailed for Callao.

14 March   HMS *Turquoise* sailed for Coquimbo, discharged W Moore[33] (clerk) to her for passage to Valparaiso (to hospital). *Hansa* sailed; *Magallanes* left blockading squadrons; the day before, she fired a couple of shots at some troops ashore.

14 March   German Corvette *Freya*[34] arrived, and a very smart looking vessel; she seemed to be very narrow and capable of steaming 16 knots; she carried 10 guns: Krupps, of moderate size about 4½ tons each.

15 March   Holbech[35] and I started at 4.30am to see if we could get any duck in the ponds beyond the *Wateree*; had some very nice sport and got 13 duck and 18 golden plover etc.

17 March   5.15am. Observed a vessel looming in the twilight and steering close under the south shore of the Morro; she turned out to be the *Union* having evaded the Blockading Squadron anchored under the lee of the forts; as soon as the blockaders

---

33   W Moore (Clerk), HMS *Turquoise*.
34   Built 1874. 2406 tons. Retired 1896.
35   Lt Edward A Holbech (1846-1915). Appointed 7 November 1877, HMS *Shannon*.

observed her the *Matias Cousino* was sent with all despatch to Ylo to fetch the *Angamos* with her long range gun and also the *Blanco* to run her off in case she attempted to escape. The *Union* brought a torpedo boat, 3 N U Gattling Guns, money for the troops and munitions of various kinds. She had just hoisted out her T-boat when at 8 am suddenly the *Cochrane* and *Amazones*[36] hove in sight from the South, they closed the blockading squadron and the place of attack was arranged; immediately the *Huascar* steered in to a range of 6,500 metres and opened fire, her shots going between the *Manco Capac* and *Union*.

The former of these two then stood out about ½ mile and opened fire at the *Huascar* After firing for some time without hitting the *Union*, she withdrew until 12.40pm when there was a general excitement and the *Cochrane* steaming in straight for the Morro the *Huascar* taking up a position 6,000 yards SW from the *Union* where the *Cochrane* got within about 4 or 5,000 yards the shot and shell began to fall uncomfortably near her and to our disgust she steered out again to a greater range. We fully expected her to run straight at the *Union* and ram her and also the *Manco Capac* for there she would have been under the guns of the Morro, or at least to go in to a range of 1,000 yards and make sure of sinking the *Union* with her shell; with her twin screws she might have kept her bows on all the time of retreat out of range, after accomplishing her mission. As it was however the firing was remarkably good from the Chileans considering the great distance and they succeeded in twice hitting the *Union*. Once she was set on fire but it was quickly put out, a second shell struck her level with the deck and passed through the funnel casing, immediately up came a dense cloud of smoke and we made sure at last she was disabled, and so thought the Chileans, for they hauled out of action having fired eighty rounds. Assembled in the offing to the northward of the Bay, the Commanders assembled on board the *Cochrane* to consult upon the next step to be taken. The *Union* now saw her opportunity and the coast clear to the South and out she dashed at full speed, having accomplished her mission.

During the action she kept up the fire from one side, and discharged cargo and

---

36   Chilean Transport.

Chorillos, 6 April 1880.

View of the Andes from the Esplanade of Chorillos showing the Bay.

coaled on the other, and it was not until 8.15pm that her opportunity arrived. The shell that struck her funnel and burst over a gun killed two men and dangerously wounded thirteen, and more or less injured thirteen more; she landed her dead and dangerously wounded men before leaving. The *Cochrane* was struck four or five times, but at such a range the damage done was nil, one shell entered abaft the battery and burst but did not kill any one; another passed through the Charthouse. The *Huascar* was struck but not damaged. Her new foremast, useless at the best of times, was struck by the *Manco Capac* and has since been removed. Since her capture by the Chileans she has been mounted with 4 x 2 deck guns, 40 pounders (probably), conning tower removed and a flying bridge put in its place and a new funnel. After Captain Thompson's death, Condell[37] of the *Covadonga* became her Captain, it was he who ran the *Independencia* ashore off Iquique.

Whilst the Commanders were quietly consulting, down rushed a Mid to report *Union* going out. In a moment a rush of the respective captains to their boats, and board their ships with the utmost speed and full cry after the *Union* but too late; they should have thought of the prospect of this happening before,when they hauled out of action and left the south open for the *Union* had the heels of them all and gave them the slip very neatly. The ships pursued but never had a change of coming in range for she started with 4.5 or 5 miles start, and 9 (pm) the chase was given up; next morning the *Angamos* and *Blanco* arrived prepared to glory in the destruction of the *Union* whom they thought caught like a rat in a hole, but to their surprise found the bird flown. They then retired again to Ylo. There is no doubt in this affair Villavicencio[38] (Capt) behaved very well and the Chileans lost their opportunity of destroying the last sea-going man-of-war belonging to the Peruvians by over-caution. The game was worth a certain amount of risk but the Chileans seemed to forget they were in Ironclads and apparently imagined themselves in wooden vessels; of what use are Ironclads to any nation if no use is made of them, if after all they are not ornamental like the old 'liners,' and it is seldom ships nowadays are opposed to guns of the poor description mounted at Arica.

---

37   Chilean; Captain Carlos Condell of *Huascar*, formerly captain of *Covadonga* and of *Independencia*.
38   Peruvian; Commandante Manuel Villavicencio (1892-1925). Captain of *Union*.

19 March   Weighed and proceeded under steam at 5.15pm, communicated with the blockading squadron.

20 March   8 am. Anchored off Ylo[39] in 19 fathoms. Anchor Bearings, West Rock off Ylo N16°30'E. Railway Chimney S62°30'E

Ylo found here the *Blanco Encalada* (Admiral Riveros[40]) *Huascar*[41], *Angamos*, *Abtao*, *Pilcomayo*[42] (the latter was captured by the *Blanco* off Mollendo sometime before and was taken to Valparaiso repaired and mounted with 6 guns, 2 of which were the long range Armstrong guns of 70 pounders). We saluted the Admiral with 13 guns.

Found the place almost denuded of troops, 4,000 only remaining, the others having been marched to Moquegua en route for Tacna and Arica and captured the place without resistance. Heard of the very serious illness of General Escala; Sotomayor[43], the War Minister, was at the front and apparently seemed to working the war himself. 11 am weighed and proceeded north.

21 March   Passed the Chilean Corvettes *Chacabuco*[44] and *Loa* standing South.

22 March   Commenced our nine hours full speed trial at 6 am.

23 March   2.30pm. Anchored in Callao Roads in six fathoms veered to two shackles. Anchor Bearings: Callao Point   88°50'W. Mole Lighthouse N82°15'E. Found here *Gannet*, *Hansa* and *Hyane*[45] German gun boats, *Garibaldi*, *Alaska* and *Decies*. The *Hyane* has a Baloon gun mounted on the . . . . one used outside Paris during the siege to fire at Baloons.

---

40   Rear Admiral Galvarino Riveros (1830-1892). Flagship *Blanco Encalada*. Chilean.
41   Damaged 27 Feb 1880.
42   Peruvian Corvette built 1873. Captured by Chileans Nov 1879. 600 tons, 180 HP.
43   General Rafael Sotomayor (1832-1880). Chilean War Minister, ?-1880.
44   Built 1867. 1670 tons. 800 HP.
45   German Gun Boat, built 1878. 570 tons. Sunk 23 July 1896.

29 March Weighed and proceeded over to San Lorenzo[46]. Made six runs with the Whitehead Torpedoes. Anchored in six fathoms.

30/31 March and 1 April Exercised rifle companies ashore firing at a target. On the 1st landed the landing party, had an attack (sham) upon one of the hills, pretty heavy work through the loose sand. Capital practice however, sorry we haven't opportunities of doing them more frequently. Had a couple of seining parties that evening; managed to get a fair haul but fouled the net over an anchor and lost good many fish and a portion of the seine. The cove near Col Harris's house is the best place but the 'Painter' was in the Bay during our stay and fish are never very plentiful when the water is white, as the natives call it, for curiously, at San Lorenzo, it has a milky appearance, whilst nearer Callao it is brown. Walked up to the lighthouse, a steep climb but the view of Callao and the Bay is very fine from it. The light itself seems to have been neglected and a small boy told me he was in charge.

3 April *Hyane* sailed.

8 April The *Victorieuse* arrived from Valparaiso.

10 April Just before daylight a loud explosion was heard on board and was immediately, or the minute after, followed by very rapid firing from the *Union* and *Oroya*. The explosion took place close to the former, immediately afterwards a steam Pinnace or Torpedo boat was seen steaming away to seaward; the bullets came flying over us pretty thickly and both the *Hansa* and *Decies* were struck. As daylight opened the smoke of vessels to the SW were seen and soon after the *Blanco*, *Huascar*, *Angamos*, *Pilcomayo* and *Matias Cousino* made their appearance. The Chileans had sent in a torpedo boat to attempt to destroy the *Union* but it was sometime before they could make out which vessel was the *Union*; they were unpleasantly near the *Alaska*

---

46   Off Callao, site of a maximum security prison.

The new neutral anchorage beyond the Rimac, a distance from Callao of around 6 miles.
S. Christobal, Lima, Monte Rico Chico, Garibaldi (Italian ship).

Ancon, 20 miles from Callao, a fashionable bathing place where the Chileans were
suspected of intending to land for a march, 'Hasta Lima'.

once or twice and finished up by seizing a fisherman and under threat of shooting him, they succeeded in having the *Union* pointed out. Unfortunately for the Chileans, the *Union* had on her seaward side spars defence. The boat, hearing daybreak being made, suspected she was being fired upon and determined to make a rush and did so and came in contact with the spars when the officer in charge pushed the firing key with no other result than shaking the *Union* pretty severely and getting pretty warmly received. Had the boat not been in such a desperate hurry to fire, they would have noticed she was unprotected except on one side and was anchored off some way from the Mole. The boat escaped without injury, and the *Union* retired behind the Mole as also the *Atahualpa*. The Chilean Admiral almost immediately afterwards notified the blockade to the shore authorities and the neutral ships by sending in a boat under a flag of truce. Eight days were given to Neutrals to clear out, the time eventually being extended to ten. The Admiral stated that, if forced to fire upon the shipping or town, due care would be taken to spare as much as possible the property of neutrals; no sooner was it known in Lima that the blockade had been established than a general exodus took place from Callao; the road to Lima was crowded with carts of every description taking all movable furniture to Lima and this continued day and night for a week; the stream of carts after this time became smaller, still the people seemed determined to remove everything likely to be destroyed by a bombardment.

The people in Lima were very uneasy on account of the *Angamos'* long-range gun and anxiously enquired whether we thought her projectiles would reach Lima; we, by the way of encouraging them, declared we felt convinced that she had the power to fire even beyond but, whether she would get orders to do so, was another matter. Lima is situated 500 feet above the level of sea and is distant from Miraflores Bay about 9,500 yards, still the elevation would be considerable to enable her (*Angamos*) to fire upon the city.

20 April   The time allowed having elapsed, the 'neutral men of war'[47] steamed down to the Rimac where we remained. The *Victorieuse,* Rear Admiral du Petit Thouars being

---

47   See watercolour page 94.

the senior, in all negotiations with the Chileans took the lead, meetings were from time to time held on board under his Presidency to settle different knotty points which might arise. Some six days before the neutral merchant vessels had cleared out of the line of fire, the PSNC steamers[48] to Ancon (en route for Chimbote) where the blockade of the place had been declared.

22 April   Considerable excitement on board for the *Huascar*, *Angamos* and *Pilcomayo* were observed cleared for action steaming in toward the town; at 2.30 they had taken up their positions: the *Huascar* and *Pilcomayo* at a range of 6,500 yards, the *Angamos* 8,000 yards; their fire was directed chiefly against the *Union* and the shipping inside the docks or camber. The firing considering the long range was particularly good especially the *Pilcomayo*'s.

She and the *Huascar* came into action with particularly large ensigns flying and the latter vessel became the object of the fire from the forts. The projectiles from the guns of these Rodman Smooth bores, most of them hardly carried halfway, and it was amusing to see the elevation they had when fired probably about 45°. This firing was particularly riling to the Peruvians for it showed them how completely they were overmatched by the superiority of the Chilean guns. It was a game of long bowls and the Chileans had every reason to be proud of the firing; several people were killed and wounded on shore, the *Union* escaping almost by a miracle, for shells kept on bursting right over her and killed two or three men but the hull was completely protected by the Darsena[49] and the Peruvians were daily building up a wall of sandbags nine deep to protect her effectively from the Northward.

The ships fired altogether 123 shots all of which fetched on shore, or amongst the shipping about 20. The shore forts [fired] about 140 but without striking the ships though several went close. In the evening at 5.30 pm the ships withdrew to San Lorenzo and an inflated account of the bombardment was put in all the papers; one went so far as to say 'at this moment 3 pm, a shot from the northward battery was seen to go almost

---

48   Pacific Steam Navigation Company founded 1838 and still sailing to South America.
49   Docks Repair Area.

Chilean Corvette O'Higgins blockading Ancon, 26 May 1880.
The Hansa can be seen to the right of the painting.

Guacolda, torpedo boat (span only) with the Blanco Encalada in the distance.

in the direction of the *Huascar'*. It clearly shows they did not expect much from their guns. Every shot fired was observed with keen interest by both officers and men on board, the rigging and yards, forward, swarming with men watching every shot fired.

23 April   At daylight, the Chileans made another attempt to blow up the *Union* and again failed. They had a tussle however with a Peruvian launch which resulted in the Peruvian boat retiring with the loss of eight men, the Chileans losing one. HMS *Turquoise* arrived from the south.

26 April   Spencer[50] (Engineer) was invalided and discharged to *Turquoise* for passage to Coquimbo. He joined at Callao and left from the same place; someone computed he had cost the country altogether since time of appointment £300. He certainly was rather a QHB, but he will no doubt be retired when he arrives in England. Le Brun[51] (Clerk) left the ship for passage to *Liffey*.

27 April   11.30 am. Weighed and proceeded for Ancon having first communicated with the blockading squadron. Anchored at Ancon[52] at 5 pm in ten fathoms. The harbour is a very snug one and the anchorage good (mud). The town is not protected in any way and being within twenty miles of Lima is just the spot for the Chileans to land if they have to take Lima; there is little or no surf and a better place for landing stores could not well be found. Still the road to Lima is commanded by high sand hills on both sides and might be well defended but the Peruvians put off everything to the last moment and no doubt think there will be time enough to protect the road when the Chileans have landed. There is a railway to Lima[53] but it is subject to so many stoppages on the way that it is hardly worth while going on it.

---

50   Discharged to HMS *Turquoise*.
51   From HMS *Shannon* to HMS *Liffey* at Coquimbo, Chile.
52   Bathing Port, twenty-two miles NW of Lima.
53   The Lima-Callao Railway was opened 17 May 1851 (one of the first in South America).

29 April   The Men's Theatrical party gave an entertainment on board 'Barts at the Swan' and the 'Two Polls'. It was a success and some ladies who were housed in one of the PSNC hulks came on board to see them; fortunate we were able to break the dull monotony of their existence. Every afternoon during our stay, we had a seining party and each time succeeded in getting good hauls of fish; rock cod, bonito, and a few flat fish; the numerous little coves are excellent for fishing and we were amply rewarded for our trouble.

1 May   We returned to Callao or rather to our old anchorage off the Rimac; found here French Flagship *Victorieuse*, *Decies*, USS *Alaska* and SMS *Hansa*. The ships were as usual rolling about in the most uncomfortable way. The *Victorieuse* must have rolled nearly 30°.

4/5/6 May   A still longer swell set in, the ships rolling very heavily; *Shannon* rolled 20°.

5 May   The *Amazones* steamed in towards the shore, too close apparently to the Forts for they opened fire upon her, she returned the fire – eight shots, but it did apparently little or no damage; she then withdrew out of range. The swell was heavy all day, and the floating dock broke adrift from her moorings and had to be sunk in 2½ fathoms of water to prevent her being knocked to pieces in the surf. Some of the Peruvian torpedoes[54] moored off the Muelle broke adrift and were noticed by the Chileans; one they fired at and destroyed, another they towed on shore at San Lorenzo and blew it up.

8 May   *Hansa* sailed for Ancon.

10 May   Sent a party on board the 'dock' to try and haul her off; the dock authorities had got everything ready: anchors laid and the water pumped out; in light draught she only drew a little over three feet of water, so there was little difficulty in hauling her

---

54   Peruvian torpedoes i.e. torpedo boats.

100

Chimbote, northern Peru, in the place where Lynch's expedition landed.

In Ferrol Bay, opposite Chimbote.

off. Thomas Roberts[55] (AB) unfortunately had his leg broken by the surging of the hawser, but Montgomerie proved equal to the occasion, set and strapped both legs together with handkerchiefs and single sticks as splints; a very bad break but the doctors hope he will recover without any material shortening of the leg. He was the smartest Royal yard man in the ship. The dock authorities behaved very well in the matter and made him a present of £50.

At 1.30 pm the Chilean ships took up their respective positions for bombardment; the *Huascar* and *Pilcomayo* 6,000 yards from the Mole V NW. The *Angamos* 10,000 yards and in almost the same line of bearing; she never came inside 8,500 yards. The *O'Higgins* was sent round the Island and took up a position 4,000 yards from the Punta and to the Southward, the *Blanco* steaming close inshore of San Lorenzo until the Punta and town were in one line and also to draw the fire of the 1,000 pounders, from the *O'Higgins*; her distance from these guns was at one time about 3,800 yards.

As soon as the vessels were in position, the *Huascar* opened fire, the other ships taking it up, the Forts replying and making much better firing than last time; shell after shell from the *O'Higgins* burst over the 1,000 pounders; short and just beyond but two at last struck one gun on the breech, the other the muzzle of the second gun; the latter ceased firing after this; but what damage was actually done, we were unable to ascertain, but one thing is certain, many men must have been disabled.

Two shots from the 1,000 pounder were fired 'almost in the direction' of the *O'Higgins* and several more at the *Blanco* to which she replied, her shot ricochetting along the Punta[56] but doing little or no damage. The fire of the other three vessels as usual was directed against the shipping and Darsena and very pretty practice it was; the *Huascar* sold the Northern fort by keeping bows on to the forts and going full speed astern, and then by turning her stern to them as though retiring out of action and again going astern, by these manoeuvres she succeeded in escaping most of the shots, she was struck however by a projectile on the Port Bow 7 feet below the waterline which penetrated the side and filled one of her compartments, another

---

55   Able Seaman Thomas Roberts, HMS *Shannon.*
56   The point or furthest land jutting into Pacific near Callao.

passed through her deck into the captain's cabin[57] and there stopped; a third hit her but without doing damage. Still no one was even wounded but so serious was the first shot that she had to retire to a greater range. Many shots from the Northern Battery passed over her and so close at times that had she had masts and yards, they would have been rattled down about decks. The *Pilcomayo* ran one or two narrow shaves of being struck but escaped. The *Angamos* was firing upon somewhere on the horn, and making good firing.

The *Blanco's* was not so successful, rather the reverse. The smooth bores on shore (excepting the Northern Battery) are not worth speaking about for their shot pitched more or less halfway. At 5.30 pm, the vessels having fired 340 shots withdrew; the 1,000 pounders firing the last shot, the Peruvians consequently claimed the victory.

Shots fired by ships:	*Blanco* (flag)	8	*Union* fired	27	(Peruvians)
(Chileans)	*Huascar*	139	Gun on Mole	19	
	Pilcomayo	108	Turret Fort	5	
	Amazones	26	North Battery	37	
	Angamos	28	Castle	6	
	O'Higgins	10	?	11	

Several people were killed and wounded on shore independently of those damaged in the Punta Battery.

12 May   Heavy swell, heavier than usual even. 3.30 am, observed the floating dock break adrift from her moorings and once more take the ground. She was sunk as before outside the surf. 11.30 am, proceeded to Ancon; found the place blockaded by the *O'Higgins*[58], communicated with her, then proceeded into harbour and anchored; found there the *Hansa*, [illegible][59] and *Decies*.

---

57   The cabin of Captain Carlos Condell, *Huascar.*
58   Ancon 26 May 1880.
59   Difficult to decipher; could be the French ship, *Hussard.*

18/19 May   Boats away from the ship clearing the merchant vessels out, the time for so doing having expired. By 4 pm not a vessel remained; all the PSNCo steamers left the day before for Chimbote[60] where they intend to establish their headquarters during the war. Every afternoon we had seining parties and had good hauls every time, in one haul we got eighty Bonito averaging 8 lbs each.

21 May   Returned to Callao, the dock authorities having telegraphed to Capt D'Arcy[61] for assistance in hauling off the dock.

22 May   5 am. Got a party of seventy men to the dock, succeeded in hauling her off and mooring her in five fathoms and this by 11am. 11.30, got under weigh and returned to Ancon being unable to land, being rolled off one's legs off the Rimac. During the middle watch, three Peruvian launches mistook one another and each thinking the other a Chilean, they opened fire, two without result, in spite of the close quarters and numerous rifle shots fired by each of them. At 2.30pm we anchored in Ancon Bay.

25 May   Received news of a torpedo action in the Bay of Callao. The two Chilean launches[62] (Thornycroft and American) were going their usual rounds, when the *Independencia* (Peruvian launch full of men) came across the Thornycroft. The Peruvian ran and the Chilean after him, the latter having the speed swung one of the outrigger torpedoes but failed to strike, she was received with a volley of musketry from the Peruvian; the officer in charge gave orders to swing out the other torpedo but

60   Northern Peruvian Port, 257 miles from Lima. Rudolph was definitely there March 1874 but perhaps also March 1872. Population 600 (1876), 140,000 (1977), 300,000 (2005)
61   Appointed 22 July 1879 HMS *Shannon*
62   Sir C Markham p.188/9 'The Chileans increased the effectiveness of the Callao blockade during the month of May by the addition of several swift torpedo-boats. Of these the *Fresia* and *Janequeo* were built by Yarrow, and sent out from England to Valparaiso in sections on board an English merchant ship, a breach of neutrality which ought to have been prevented. It is sad to reflect how very little harm these misguided countries could have done to each other if it had not been for the same means of destruction supplied to them by England, Germany and the United States. The *Fresia* and *Janequeo* were of steel, with five watertight compartments, seventy feet long, and with a speed of eighteen knots. The *Janequeo* was fitted with three McEvoy patent duplex outrigger torpedoes, one on a boom rigged out on the stern, the others on side-swinging booms; the two boats also carried a Hotchkiss machine gun each.'

somehow the order was never obeyed. This officer thought the torpedo had been swung out (why?) and pressed the firing key.

Up went the Peruvian, but unfortunately so did the Chilean. The other Peruvian boats made off for the Mole leaving their comrades to drown. The Chileans swam off to a lighter where they remained until picked up by the other launch; this boat succeeded in capturing the officer in charge, Galvez[63], and six or eight men; the remainder, ten in number, were drowned as also two Chileans.

Galvez was found to be so badly wounded, that Admiral Riveros gave leave for him to be sent on shore on parole; after a day or two when he had partly recovered, he was 'interviewed' and stated he blew up the Chileans with a shot from his revolver fired at the torpedo lying on her deck and also, to make double sure, had thrown another on board with a time fuse! He also stated, when at the bottom of the sea, he recognised Ugarte[64] the other officer, who was drowned. It was a pitch dark night and how he could have seen the torpedo in the Chilean boat at all is incredible, still more so the 'Ugarte' yarn. Since that time, he had not been recovering so fast and can it be wondered at after putting...... and Saphira in the Shade completely, I wonder he was not afraid of getting a like fate. On the strength of all these gallant deeds, Pierola instituted an order of 1st and 2nd class 'heroes'. Galvez was made a 1st class one, the late Almirante Grau one of the 2nd Class. What can be thought of a country which has two kinds of heroes, but it is said everyone is a hero so it is necessary to draw the distinction somewhere. Sent the steam pinnace to Chancay for mails; she ran the distance in two hours.

In the evening there was farewell reception on board the *Hansa*, she having been ordered home. The *Hansa* and ourselves were great friends and a hard-working lot they were. There is no doubt the Germans are thoroughly in earnest and intend to make their officers and men (if possible) decidedly efficient, it was amusing to hear the Frenchman ask whether we considered they (Germans) were improving. The officers of these two nations have no intercourse. The captains alone doing the strictly formal and necessary calls. Every day the *Hansa*'s did something in the way of drill and, until this is over, no officer is allowed on shore.

---

63   Lt Jose Galvez M (1850-1894), Peruvian.
64   Col. Alfonso Ugarte (1847-1880), Peruvian hero.

26 May   Returned to Callao, anchored off Rimac: *Alaska* and *Garibaldi* were both here.

27 May   Observed a party of Peruvian divers at work over the wreck of Chilean torpedo boat: the *Huascar* seeing them opened fire upon the divers who quickly returned in their boats to shore, she then fired upon the shipping and at 11 am she was joined by the *Angamos* who fired a few shots on chance of disabling the *Union*; at 12.15 the ships withdrew having fired twenty-three shots. The shore batteries replied with seventy-five shots which did no harm.

The *Union* was set on fire in two places and the jib boom of one of the Peruvian vessels knocked out. Before the *Huascar* opened fire, she communicated with us and stated the Hulks etc. were in the way of their fire and asked us to move them which we accordingly did, about half of a mile further away from the town. The Peruvian divers and boats made a point, whilst carrying on their attempt to raise the torpedo boat, of hiding themselves amongst the neutral hulks, so very naturally the Chileans asked us to get them removed.

The same night, the Chileans sent in their other torpedo boat and diver who went down and placed 100 lbs of dynamite inside the boat. The Chileans having fired the charge withdrew, the diver ascertained the boat had already been slung ready for raising, so the Chileans were only just in time – destroying her.

29 May   Daylight. Peruvian boats hard at work at the wreck little thinking the boat (torpedo) had been destroyed the previous night. The remaining Chilean on the watch, made a dash at the Peruvian boats and drove them away but she herself was set upon by several other boats full of men and had to retire, the shore forts firing at her. The *Angamos*, *Huascar* and *Pilcomayo* at once got into position and opened fire upon the shipping. At 9 am the firing ceased the ships hauled out of action.

The *Huascar* fired	21	Shore batteries fired only 34 shots finding
Pilcomayo	61	the vessels out of range.
Angamos	<u>13</u>	
	95	

The mean distance of the ships from the shore was 7,800 yards. The firing was beautiful and I had a good opportunity of judging being on shore at the time, having come down from Lima to go on board to keep the forenoon watch – I heard several shots on the way down, and saw the ships getting into position. I suspected the Gig would not be in for me but felt compelled to walk down to the camber to see, the train having stopped at Bella Vista: one shell burst within a 100 yards of the train (from the *Angamos*) and blew up a mud hut. Noticing several people walking towards the Mole, I followed and found a crowd assembled to see the firing and in the highest of spirits, evidently they thought a bombardment good fun with no danger attached to it. I felt convinced the Chileans only fired at the shipping and, knowing what good shots they made, knew it was pretty safe on the Mole near the Camber.

Shell after shell fell in the basin; one struck the *Tumbes*[65] sailing Corvette at the waterline under the main chains and in three or four minutes down she went; she first began to roll slightly, then to pitch, a heavy forward lurch and she sank in the Shoal water with her stern and starboard netting just visible. A large hulk full of coal was also struck and sank in a short time, her coal a heavy loss for the Peruvians, who have not too large a stock of it.

She remained with her lower masts just above the water. Several shells (about a dozen altogether) pitched in the sand bag defence of the *Union* and *Oroya* and failed to penetrate more than three bags deep, the defence being nine deep.

Some passed over the shipping and bursting destroyed a few houses, but the damage done was very little. The *Union* for a long time had been getting her new guns on board (two (said to be) 12 ton guns) and from behind her fortification she replied to the Chilean ships; but without result, one of the *Pilcomayo*'s shell, burst right over her, but did no damage, several more passed over the hurricane deck of the *Oroya,* one bursting and blowing up an engine used for working a crane, but no one was damaged.

One shell burst inside the Camber and at once there was a rush to get into 'better quarters,' myself amongst the number; I got a capital view from the top of a building

---

65   Peruvian Corvette. Sank Callao 29 May 1880.

Oroya railway bridge over the Rimac, showing Horse Shoe Tunnel.

just in front of the Club[66]. The enthusiasm of the heroic Peruvians attained its greatest height when they noticed the *Atahualpa* getting under weigh and steaming out from the docks accompanied by a tug; she was going out to fight the Chileans single handed, so said the lookers on, and out she steamed towards the vessels but after steaming about half of a mile from the Mole she changed her mind and slowly returned to her old place.

She made a 'great smoke' and this seemed to 'fetch' the Peruvians who expected wonders out of it, but nothing came; at this moment the Chileans no doubt thought they had fired enough for they also withdrew from action. The 'heroes' now cheered for the very sight of the *Atahualpa* had driven the cowardly Chileans away. Astounding they should be able to pull themselves to such an extent.

1 June   The 'Glorious 1st of June,' doubly so for the *Shannon*'s brought good news to the Chileans by the *Princess Louise*[67] (a mail steamer) for heavy fighting had taken place and Tacna had fallen. The Bolivians had retired to La Paz[68]; Montero[69] with a comparatively small body of men on Tarata[70] en route for Arequipa[71], leaving the way open to Arica; this blow was doubly crushing to the Peruvians for they fully expected to hear of a victory in the south; for only a short time before L'Escala had resigned and Sotomayor, the Minister of War, had died suddenly and it was supposed, before anything further could be done, the former would have to return. Baquedano[72] however took charge and soon showed he was equal to the occasion and intended to have no more 'manana,' the result as before stated.

The Chileans thus (it was supposed) without a chief, an army without a head, would soon cease to exist in the face of the intrepid 'heroes' they would have to encounter; but so much for human hopes, so sadly dispelled. About this time, the Cabinet held a meeting as to whether neutral ships (men of war) should be allowed to remain in their waters! This was notoriously a hit at the *Shannon* who was accused of provisioning the

66   The Club, Callao.
67   Mail steamer probably Chilean.
68   Capital of Bolivia. Population 30,000 (1876), 800,000 (1977), 1,250,000 (2005). Highest capital in the world; 11,700 feet.
69   Rear Admiral Lizardo Montero (1832-1905), Vice President of Peru. (see page 121)
70   Battle ground city.
71   Third city of Peru: 635 miles south of Lima. Population 29,250 (1876), 225,000 (1977), 650,000 (2005). Altitude: 7661 feet.
72   Chilean; General Manuel Baquedano (1826-1897).

Chilean vessels etc, but eventually they were considerate enough graciously to permit us to remain. To have informed us [that] no more provisions could be permitted to leave the shore would have been quite legitimate, for the blockade had been established for some time and we were rather surprised they did not do so. A party of officers from the ship went up to Chicla for three days leave to try the ascent of Mt Meiggs[73].

When the Line[74] was first begun wonders were expected from it, the whole country was to be opened out, mines hitherto unworked were to be started and unmeasured wealth was to flow into the country; even the Andes were to be no check, for the railway was to surmount these and, passing down the other side, connect the Eastern towns of Peru with Lima.

In actual fact, the Railway[75] is one of the wonders of the world and is actually in working order as far as Chicla at an elevation of 12,200 feet but, as far as one can hear, all it has done has been to mount up the National Debt and will never repay the millions sunk into it originally for there is no country to open out. From Lima upwards, it is nothing but one range of mountains in succession to another until the summit of the Cordilleras is reached. The valleys are wonderfully fertile and even the mountain sides to this day bear witness to the wonderful system of irrigation pursued by the Incas. When the Spaniards first landed they made it their boast that . . . . Conquerors might cultivate the valleys, they would turn the mountains to account and so they did. One thing strikes one forcibly and this is the depopulation of the county. The whole valley of the Rimac as far as Chicla and even in some places beyond to this day show traces of the industry of the Incas but, expecting the few modern towns or villages on the line, there is hardly a sign of a hut existing. The natives (Indians) uneducated, perhaps not knowing even where Chile was, were drawn away wholesale for soldiers and in many cases were lassoed and brought down in gangs from the mountains to Lima. Hardly a gang came down without an attempt of some at least to escape and usually they were

---

73   Named after Henry Meiggs (1811-1877) an American who began the world-famous and impressive Andean Railway.
74   The main line of the central railway, from Callao to Huancayo, is 224 miles; 107 miles from the coast it crosses the Andes at 15,688 feet. It is the highest gauge line in the world. It was financed – and until recently – owned by the (British) Peruvian Corporation – and built mostly by imported Chinese labour between 1870 and 1893.
75   Rudolph describes the railway very well but has different heights for the Summit Tunnel.

La Oroya, Oroya railway.

The Oroya Railway running alongside San Mateo, one of the villages
in the valley of the Rimac.

unsuccessful, the renegades being shot down – and these men are Peru's volunteers. The Peruvians themselves (of Spanish origin) were content to remain at home and plot further revolutions to fighting unless forced to do so before Lima itself.

The Railway was built up by Meiggs, he having obtained subsidies from the Government for the purpose. As far as San Bartolome[76], it is nothing more than a steady incline following the line of the Rimac[77] with barren rocky hills on either side; at this point there is some attempt at cultivation and the potatoes grown here and Matucana[78] are famous. From San Bartolome, the Railway winds about round one hill and back again to the same point (at least so it seems until one finds oneself some seventy or eighty feet above the line one started from) at one point near this place two tunnels (one exactly above the other) are to be seen on the face of the hill with the Railway below; in other words three parallels or zigzags. The Virrugas bridge, iron and apparently of too slight a structure about 300 feet long and about 200 feet higher spanning the two tunnels. Matucana at an elevation of 7,800 feet, a very pretty place with a decent hotel, is a very pleasant place to stay a few days away from the ship; the climate here is delightfully cool, and the mountain sides at this place assume a greenish appearance for the first time after leaving Lima which makes it doubly agreeable. Tambo-de-Viso (8,900) the scene of the great land slip a few months ago when three complete sets of rails were utterly destroyed by the whole mountain side coming down with the run and precipitating itself into the bed of the Rimac below, which here is nothing but a mountain torrent. A train passed over the VV[79] not an hour before the slip took place; I happened to be staying at Matucana at the time and rushed out to see the slip. It (railway) seemed so thoroughly destroyed that months would elapse it was thought before it could be repaired, but it was in working order under three.

San Mateo[80] is the largest place on the line but is really nothing more than a large village situated in a valley with mountains all round, and the river running through it,

---

76   Railway village at about 5,000 feet.
77   Andean river crossing Lima.
78   Railway village at 7,838 feet and 52 miles from Lima.
79   'VV' appears to describe the zig-zags in the line.
80   Town at over 10,000 feet and 63 miles from Lima. A well known bottle mineral water comes from here.

the line sides are all beautifully cultivated and irrigated and the town or village has a few very decent buildings, the chief one of course being the church, rather imposing with its massive front and two large towers, but the chief object of interest is the Infiernello Bridge[81] (10,294) spanning a wide chasm in the mountains. Just before reaching it the line is circuitous, winding round hill sides out of one tunnel into another, so sharp the turns being that frequently one loses sight of the engine from the fourth carriage, at times the train rushes along the bare edge of a cliff, precipitous and hundreds of feet below rushes the foaming torrent. All at once a tunnel is entered and in a few moments the wonder of this remarkable railway is reached, the train passes over the swinging bridge and once more dives out of sight into another tunnel and once more into the open through a succession of tunnels and upwards once more to VV[82] (11,100) where the scenery is magnificent; and where for the first time the streaks of snow show the elevation being reached. Near this spot is a celebrated silver mine but not worked owing to the want of labour, thirty yards of a glacier had to be penetrated to work it and so precipitous is it that llamas[83] alone are able even up the zigzag path to carry the ore below. A peculiarity about these animals is they never will carry a pound or more than a quintal (100 lbs) and should any more be placed on their backs they lay down and will rather die than move another step. They are beautiful looking animals, very clean built and most dignified and add greatly to the landscape for in some places herds of them are seen grazing on the mountain sides. They vary very much in colour, but varieties of browns are the predominant colours.

Chicla[84] (12,200) is the highest point at present worked by the railway, but the road is actually made as far as the Summit Tunnel[85] (15,700) and is in construction to Oroya[86] on the eastern side of the Andes. There is a marked difference in climate once Chicla is reached, the air being much more rarified. There is a very decent hotel kept by W.

81 This bridge is 65 miles from Lima at an altitude of 11,100 feet
82 Zig-zag railway.
83 Peruvian National Animal.
84 Current altitude is given as 12,251 feet and 71 miles from Lima.
85 See watercolour page 119.
86 This large mining town is at 12.178 feet and is 117 miles from Lima. Population 140 (1876), 35,000 (1977), 36,000 (2005).

Chicla, the highest point of the Oroya Railway, looking down
upon the station (12,202 ft).

Summits of the Andes, as seen from near the
Summit Tunnel (c15,200 ft).

Schultz (a German) very reasonable with the only expensive items, the guide and horses. He escorted us up to the Summit Tunnel himself where we found all work had been discontinued; a solitary Cornishman being the only person in charge of the place. He put up our horses and we started up Mt Meiggs only 2,000 feet above us. The rarification of the atmosphere was the chief obstacle but Heyman[87] and myself managed to get up in thirty-eight minutes and down in twenty-one. There was a cross upon the top which we desecrated with our names and the *Shannon*'s. The view from the summit well repays the slight inconvenience of a 'headache' which we got from walking up fast, range after range, each in succession lower than the preceding one, varied in colour and all capped with snow, a clear blue sky overhead with a bright sun lighting up the snow clad mountains intensifying the varied colours of the rock and sandstone upon their sides, as far as the eye could reach the rugged peaks extended until lost in the distance on the eastern side of the Andes and there one felt how at last one had reached the summit of them. Upon the slope of the range (of which Mt Meiggs is one) there are three parallels of lagoons with beautifully green grass on their edges, one above the other and said to abound with wildfowl, but unfortunately our guns we had left on board and one requires a couple of days or so to get accustomed to the climate.

The ride is most interesting to the Summit Tunnel along a winding and circuitous path sufficiently wide in places for one horse only to pass, and one has to keep a good look out to see before coming to the ledges whether anybody is starting from the other end for one or the other must go over. In some places the track is cut in the side of the face of the mountain and for hundreds of feet is a sheer precipitous descent with the rushing mountain torrent of the Rimac below. One, however, even in this wild country finds a place of refreshment in a snug little valley where there is an Indian village which boasts of a hotel kept by an Italian, where breakfast or dinner is provided with wine of the country, whilst the walls are decorated with the pictures of the Duilio, Dandolo[88] etc, all ready for battle and making plenty of smoke. One meets or rather sees up the hill sides herds of the llamas grazing quietly and waiting to be driven into the

---

87   Gerald A Heyman, Midshipman appointed 10 Jan 1878, HMS *Shannon*.
88   One day, this can perhaps be explained.

corrals and loaded with silver ore. It is no uncommon thing to meet a small sturdy Indian lad of probably not more than twelve years driving a herd of perhaps two or three hundred llamas before him and conducting them perfectly along the mountain passes.

The horses seemed to feel the rarification more than we did, but were accustomed to it for one had to be careful lest the animal should drop down exhausted. One of our party had a very narrow escape meeting upon one of the narrow ledges some miles but fortunately in the centre there was sufficient room for his horse to back into the rock though at one time his hindquarters were actually over the ledge, and he was just able to recover himself by a supreme effort. We were wonderfully fortunate in getting the view we did for soon the drizzling rain and driving clouds came on and completely hid the mountain summit from our sight. We were not sorry when we got back to our hotel and were able to talk of the trip of the day now the pressure upon our heads was reduced and we were able to enjoy a fair meal. Next morning a sharp frost, but stern duty made us pack up and be off by the train for Lima and our ship. No steam is used on the return journey except at the VVs and beyond Matucana when the road has a slighter gradient; there is always a certain percentage of danger from falling rocks etc and our train was no exception for, when we were within a few miles of Chosica[89], we had to stop for a huge rock came down and completely blocked the line. A number of workmen were soon on the spot and in a couple of hours the line was clear; the engine towing the rock along the line until it was finally thrown into the Rimac which valley the Railway follows as far as Tambo de Viso[90].

Found great excitement in Lima at the news of the defeat down South, so unexpected for they knew their ships were not equal to the Chileans, but their men ....! But of course it was the foreign element which had managed the trick for the Chileans. Pierola now started his men making the defences for Lima, utilising the

---

89   Popular winter resort. Twenty-five miles east from Lima and nearly 3,000 feet. Rudolph had some fun here: *Memoirs* p.100/1 'As I always travel on the top of the cars, so as to enjoy the scenery, I got on to the engine with two of our party, and reached Chosica before the people in the train knew why they had been left behind. At the hotel we found a family of Americans, three of them very pretty girls, so having introduced myself, and finding a piano and music, I proposed at this unearthly hour (9am) a dance outside, which we had until the new engine arrived from Lima, and brought the train up. We had several songs, and altogether we had 'a good time' as the young ladies called it.'
90   Tambo de Viso

Summit Tunnel, c15,200 feet, highest point of the Oroya Railway: line
only laid, traffic working no further than Chicla (12,200).
Mt Meiggs to the right of the painting, 17,574 ft.

sand hills on the plain facing Chorillos[91] and the construction of the lines of Miraflores[92], hundreds of men were employed and an English firm (White) were ordered to construct Cannon which should place the Peruvians on some par with their enemy who had Krupp and Gatling Guns.

The Archbishop[93] permitted the church bells to be given up for the construction of cannon and defence of Lima and arms were poured into the country through the unblockaded ports to the north and brought overland to the capital (Peabody, Martin[94]) in fact, everything was done to give the enemy as good a reception as possible in front of the Capital: everybody was more or less a soldier and everybody felt proud of belonging to the Reserva fondly hoping they would never be called into action. The numbers of officers increased to an alarming extent and seemed more content in lounging about smoking cigarettes and drinking to studying tactics; no uncommon thing to see a hero of 16 Captain of a company, knowing as much about the company as they did of the prominent part they might soon be called upon to play. New pattern caps in which all the colours of the rainbow existed with the Sun of Peru for a badge were to be seen and not a sword was to be had in Lima, so great was the demand from these defenders of the soil.

12 June   HM Ships *Thetis* and *Turquoise* arrived from the South. The weather during the latter part of our stay was decidedly unpleasant, overcast, gloomy with drizzling rain which is called 'dew'[95] in Callao, with thick fog at times, but as a rule the weather cleared when the sea breeze set in, which it persistently did about 11 am. In our different anchorage off the Rimac, we had one advantage over the nearer ones, we avoided the 'Painter'.

15 June   *Gannet* sailed.

---

91   Residential town a few miles south of Lima; (page 90) pen and ink, actually drawn and signed 6 April 1880.
92   Residential coastal suburb of Lima.
93   Monsignor Francisco Orueta y Castrillon, Archbishop of Lima.
94   The American H O Peabody was granted a U.S. patent for his rifle mechanism in 1862.
95   'Dew' in Callao. The Peruvians call it 'Garúa'

22 June   The *Penguin* arrived.

25 June   Exercised at General Quarters and making runs with the *Whitehead* torpedoes. The last we fired ran 100 yards from the ship and then sank.

26 June   Target practice in the afternoon.

28 June   Strong breeze with a chopping sea.

30 June   Passed Ylo.

1 July   7 am. Anchored off Arica[96] in eleven fathoms, found the place under Chilean colours, the *Abtao,* a couple of transports and Peruvian ditto at Anchor, the latter had come down under the protection of the 'Red Cross Flag'[97] for wounded Peruvians and the bodies of Bolognesi[98], More, etc, who fell defending the Morro. Three of our officers went up to Tacna to see the battlefield and rode over it accompanied by a Chilean officer. They reported, considering the time Montero had had at his disposal, the defences were wretched and much time had been wasted in making the rear of them as strong as the front. The Peruvians and Bolivians numbered about ...000 men; the former on the right, the latter the left; the Chilean army actually brought into contact with the enemy was probably never more than 11,500 men; their cavalry was of little or no use through want of handling and the heaviness of the ground (sand).

The Peruvians never stood their ground at all and all the way to Tacna the place was strewn with arms and munitions of war; the Bolivians marked the ground they had held with their bodies and they seem to have fought pluckily. But all through this war, the Peruvians have been lamentably deficient in artillery though it is true they had some four Krupp and Gatling Guns but these were all taken in the early part of the day. Montero[99] was one of the first to arrive at Tacna accompanied by a large staff whilst the

---

96   They had been there 2-10 November 1879.
97   The Red Cross was founded 1864 in Geneva.
98   Bolognesi and More died 7 June 1880.
99   Rear Admiral Lizardo Montero (1832-1905). Vice President of Peru. (see page 109)

General view of Arica and neighbouring country after the storming by the Chileans.

battle was going on, but Campero[100] (Bolivian) remained to the last and lost several or the majority of his staff and returned almost alone. When the rout once began, had the Chileans made better use of their Cavalry, the Peruvian troops would have been destroyed or captured but, as it was, a great number were able to retreat upon Arequipa.

The Bolivians were utterly disgusted with their allies and declared they would fight no more with them and quietly disbanded and returned to La Paz and the interior. Baquedano commanded the Chileans and had 18,000 men landed at Ylo on their way to Tacna. The Moquegua Valley had been scoured and a heavy contribution exacted; the

---

100 Presidente Narciso Campero (1815-1896), President of Bolivia 1880-1884

heights of Los Angeles stormed with but slight loss and other minor engagements taken place and always with success to the Chilean arms. During our stay, Valdivieso, Commandant of Arica, provided us with horses and did all in his power to make us enjoy our visit and one day the Chileans brought out twenty-four guns to practise at the 'Wateree'[101] – they certainly made excellent practice firing as they were at 4,000 yards; they have eight horses to each gun and eight mules to each Gatling. Arica itself, when once attacked, only resisted for rather more than an hour. The Cavalry were posted to cut off the Peruvian retreat by the Sorata Valley, Artillery upon the hills upon the north side of it (distance about 4,500 yards from the nearest redoubt) whilst the Infantry took up positions to the southward. The 3rd and 4th Regiments were told off to march and take up their positions to the southward of the two outlying redoubts during the night

---

101 *Wateree*, a wreck, see page 64, note 53.

which they did and within a few hundred yards of them as the Peruvians had no outposts and consequently no idea of their enemy's vicinity. The Cazadores (Chasseurs) took up their position towards the Camarones Valley.

(7 June)   The *Thetis* was present during the attack. An officer thus describes it: 'At 6.45 am 7 June a Gun was fired from above the Sorata Valley as a signal for attack: dawn was just breaking and in a moment the sand hills near the Redoubts were lined with skirmishers where not a man had before been seen or expected by the Peruvians: they only had time to fire their guns from the redoubts once or twice before the regiments swept them out bayoneting everyone who remained, more than 400 died in the SE redoubt, they (3rd and 4th) had orders to await further instructions but without waiting they fixed bayonets and rushed the Morro, killing Bolognesi[102] and Moore (late Captain of the *Independencia*). Many of the heroic Peruvians, rather than face the Chileans' bayonets, leapt into the sea and for this their memory was eulogised in Lima as worthy of their country and so they were. The men who were not killed on the Morro ran down into the town where they were all butchered later on. One of the redoubts was blown up by Moore thinking it had been deserted by the Peruvians and occupied by the Chileans and he managed to destroy over 300 of his own men.'

Baquedano sent in two messages demanding the surrender of the place as further resistance he assured them was useless, but Bolognesi answered the usual thing 'until the last cartridge was fired etc' and paid the penalty; he and Moore seem to have acted gallantly. When the Morro was rushed, the Chileans fired down upon the top of the *Manco Capac* who immediately got underweigh into deep water where she was sunk by her Commander,[103] the crew escaping in the boats. They vainly endeavoured to get aboard the neutral ships but failed and eventually were taken prisoners and placed on board a transport going South.

---

102   Col Francisco Bolognesi (1816-1880), Peruvian hero.
103   Peruvian; Commander Captain Jose Sanchez Marsino

Bay of Coquimbo from the signal station showing view of the Andes. In the bay are La Serena, storeship Liffey, Shannon, Gannet, Amazones and Nereus (late storeship).

The ships during the land attack assisted by shelling the Morro and North forts; the latter was destroyed by the Peruvians before deserting there, an enormous trench had been dug across the valley in the rear of the town and this the Chileans were expected to attack but they did not, to the Peruvians' disgust. About 1,200 Peruvians were killed and some four or five hundred Chileans; few prisoners were taken and wounded were not many on the Peruvian side. We all thought the *Manco* would have in the last extremity, closed with the *Cochrane* but her Commander seemed to think otherwise.

I shot a few duck during our stay but they were not at all plentiful and very wild. We had however some capital lawn tennis upon an asphalt court inside the station. A large part of the town near the Morro was utterly destroyed but some of the principal buildings remained intact; the Peruvians mined the church but somehow it was not blown up.

4 August   6 am. Sailed for Iquique and arrived next day at 8.30am, found a cricket match arranged, went on shore and got beaten. They made 64 to our 34, but in the 2nd innings we were more fortunate but had no time to finish the match; we left the same evening.

9 August   8.40 pm. Anchored in 8½ fathoms in Coquimbo Bay. During our stay we had a succession of northerly winds accompanied by rain and fog but the weather was delightfully cool after Peru.

11 August   A fresh norther (force 7) suddenly came on during the middle watch and we dragged nearly down to the *Dover Castle*[104]; let go a second anchor but the first held the ship all right and was a Mactues Anchor. The rains have been heavier than known for years and have washed away the river bridge between Serena and Compania besides doing other damage.

12 August   Another strong norther but it lasted for two hours only accompanied by heavy rains, inland much damage done and the course of the river changed.

15 August   Very severe earthquake lasting 1½ minutes making the ship quiver as though in collision. The town of Mafred half way to Valparaiso almost entirely destroyed. HMS *Osprey* anchored. Whilst here, we heard of the destruction of the *Loa* off Callao. She saw a schooner at anchor about three miles from the shore and a boat put off to board her; she sent in a boat to capture the Peruvian who immediately pulled on shore and bolted; the *Loa*'s boat took the other in tow noticing her to be full of provisions.

The captain ordered her alongside to get the vegetables out (though he had been expressly warned against a boat of this description), the 1st Lieut even expostulated

---

104   British Wreck.

with him – the captain enforced his order and, after a box or two of vegetables had been passed up the side, the boat suddenly exploded blowing the *Loa*'s side right in and in 3 minutes she had sunk with the top of her masts above the water. The neutral ships had seen the occurrence and sent their boats; the *Thetis*'s being on the spot first. They succeeded in saving about 40 men, the remainder, the captain included, were drowned. Captain D'Arcy had been very unwell for some time so went down to hospital at Valparaiso by Mail.

18 August   We left for Valparaiso where we anchored on the 20th.

20 August   And took up the *Almirante Cochrane*'s moorings. The anchors were each of 4 tons (north and south) 2 inch ground chain and 2½ inch pendant. We shackled our cable to the Pendant and sent the buoy to the Hulk. During our stay, weather overcast and heavy swell from the northward with an awkward wash on the beach for landing.

22 August   A heavy norther came on bringing in a heavy swell but we were well protected so avoided a good deal of the motion we otherwise should have had. By 11 am it was blowing 6 to 7 upsteam, let go BB underfoot. Barometer 30.29, by 1 pm the weather began to clear; by 5 it had fallen, weighed BB, drew fires at 10 pm. With the northers, the barometer rises before they come on. During our stay, the weather on the whole was very pleasant, sea breeze coming in about 11 am and lasting until the evening.

Valparaiso

28 August   Had another norther this time. The bar fell; overcast weather and swell, not much wind.

7 September   Capt D'Arcy rejoined, before we left, from hospital where he had been dangerously ill. A few days before we sailed, in sending down top masts, Smith (AB)[105]

---

105   Able Seaman Smith (?-1880).

fell from aloft and was instantly killed. He was buried the next day in C of E cemetery on shore; the Chileans were much struck by the funeral and the papers made comments upon it; he was a smart young fellow and his loss much regretted. PM slipped our moorings and proceeded under steam.

8 September   8.30 pm. Passed the *Huascar* steering South. We left at sick quarters, Stileman (act Sub) and Pearce[106] (mid).

9 September   11 am. Arrived and anchored in Coquimbo Bay. Remained here until the 20th.

19 September   On the 19th we heard of the destruction of the *Covadonga*[107], she was a sloop of 412 tons, 180 HP, captured from the Spaniards in 1866, she carried 2 x 70 pounder Armstrong and 3 small guns, Capt S Ferri[108]. The following description was given by an Englishman, a seaman on board:

> (13 September) 'She entered the Port of Chancay and opened fire upon the Railway without however destroying it; whilst in the bay, she observed two boats at anchor; she immediately lowered a boat to destroy them which she did in the case of one but the other being a smart looking gig with airtight boxes cushions etc, was brought off to the ship.'

The carpenter was sent into her to examine her and discovered nothing wrong so the captain determined to appropriate her to his own use and ordered her to be hoisted up she having chain slings fitted all ready. These led through two pipes in the foremost and after air chambers, the fall were hauled taut and order 'Hoist Away' given when the firing gear of the torpedo[109] was released and off it went with a tremendous explosion.

---

106   Henry L D Pearce, Midshipman. Appointed 30 November 1878, HMS *Shannon*.
107   Chilean sloop captured from Spain 1866, sunk Chancay, Peru, 13 September 1880.
108   Chilean.
109   Rudolph went on a torpedo course in 1881. He then wrote a manuscript "*Disadvantages of Frictional Electricity for Torpedo Purposes*".

The starboard side of the *Covadonga* was blown right in, her foreyard fell with a crash and in four minutes she sank in ten fathoms of water, fifteen men escaped in the Gig, (the dinghy, the only other uninjured boat being swamped from overcrowding) and reached the *Pilcomayo* which was blockading Ancon. Forty-nine were taken prisoners, the remainder perished.

The Plains near the town of Coquimbo during the months of August and September are covered with wild flowers; it is astounding how a few days rain seem to completely alter the sandy looking ground. We had good dove shooting and got a few snipe but it was hard work with little result.

20 September   We sailed from Coquimbo; had torpedo practice and a number of people from Compania and Coquimbo came on board to see it. We returned about 1pm and weighed again at 4pm.

21/22 September   Exercised at prize firing in the forenoon each day but the firing was decidedly bad.

26 September   7.30 am. Arrived and anchored off Iquique. Played the return match with ICC (Iquique Cricket Club); we went in first and made 98 and Iquique 53, 2nd innings *Shannon*'s 135 (R de L: 28 and 25).

28 September   Played another return match, Iquique 32 and 79, *Shannon* 66 unable to finish innings (R de L: 0). In the evening we were invited to a grand ball given by Mr North, our band having been lent for the occasion; about sixty men made their appearance and three ladies. The Peruvian ladies were afraid of meeting Chilean ones and some of the latter authorities were frightened out of attending by our gold lace (epaulettes and gold lace trousers). The dance turned out a debauch in which a fabulous amount of liquid was consumed and very little dancing done, I danced all of the evening without stopping until a perfect pulp, but most of the men showed Iquique had not lost its reputation for wetness whatever its otherwise sandy and dreary appearance might lead a stranger to think.

"Huacho" on his native hills near Iquique; a Guanaco

30 September   It is only fair to add, Mr and Mrs North did their best but were sold through the mutual dislike of their invited guests.

1 October   6.30 pm. Sailed from Iquique, called at Pisagua to communicate with the English Vice Consul; 7.30 arrived and anchored off Arica, found the *Abtao* and several transports all ready for embarking the Chilean expedition for Lima.

Note:
Manco Capac[110]; she lies in eight fathoms, on her starb side heeled and NNE; least water over her funnel 5¾ fathoms; her turret has fallen out and upside down. Her position as follows by angles taken over her funnel.

Position:		
W Summit Alacran	Anchorage 28° Church 37°58'	
Q Railway bridge	87°65'	
Wateree – Bearing of Church	S12°55'E	

6 October   *Lackawanna*[111] arrived with Mr Christiancy[112] to arrange, if possible, terms of peace. For some reason or other the *Chalaco* had put into Mollendo being unable to come into Arica on account of the Chilean flag being hoisted! As if they did not, it was when they started. The Chilean and Bolivian authorities having arrived, the Chilean Minister of War (Vergara)[113] sent to say if the *Chalaco* did not arrive in three days, he would begin embarking for Lima; this seemed to have the desired effect for in two days she made her appearance.

22 October   First meeting took place 22 October where they agreed to have a final one on the 25th.

---

110   Peruvian Ironclad, scuttled Arica, 7 June 1880.
111   American frigate, built 1862, 3000tons, sold 1887.
112   US Minister Isaac P Christiancy (?-?).
113   General Jose Francesco Vergara (1833-1889), Minister of War.

23 October   On the 23rd we heard Iquique was on fire and nearly destroyed; so on the 24th we steamed down to the place and anchored at 5 pm same evening.

Anchor Bearings:	L	H	S11°30'E
	Punta	Negra	N54°E

Found here *Huascar* and French sloop *Hussard*, the latter had done good work at the fire and saved a large amount of property; the Chilean soldiers had availed themselves of the opportunity to pillage.

Iquique

Thirty blocks were destroyed, the pavements (all new since the Chilean occupation) burnt; about four fifths of the town destroyed.

25 October   We left in the evening for Callao. The Conference ended as the Chileans expected – no result. The Peruvians seemed to have thought words and argument would settle the whole business and treated the Chileans as though they had been victorious and were dictating terms to Chile. Tarapaca was the bone of discussion; the Peruvians would not hear of it and talked of their invincible position at Lima; so it fell through. The Chileans hurrying on their preparations for the final part of the campaign.

30 October   Arrived and anchored in twelve fathoms off the Rimac in Callao Bay.

Anchor Bearings:	Lorenzo Pt	S46°W
	Callao Pt	S13°30E

Found here Italian ships *Garibaldi*, *Archimedo*[114], German *Ariadne*[115], French *Decies*, US *Adams*[116]. Chilean squadron were off the port blockading; the three Ironclads and *O'Higgins*.

---

114   Italian ship built ?
115   German Corvette, built 1871, 2072 tons, retired 1891.
116   US Corvette, built Boston 1876, 1400 tons, sold 1920.

1 November   The *Osprey*, *Lackawanna* and *Chalaco* arrived confirming the previous report of the end of the Conference.

8 November   We embarked 300 people mostly women and children from Chorillos. Lieut Garreton (Garezon?)[117] (Nav. of the *Atahualpa*) came round in us to steer the ship clear of torpedoes which I don't believe for an instance exist.

I was sent on shore to do the embarking and met the Magues who were leaving the country for Paris; they had to pay no less than £10,000 to Pierola before they were allowed to leave the country. We took all the people to the head of San Lorenzo and turned them over to the *Santa Rosa*. Most of the passengers were very unwell, though there was only slight motion. 6.40 pm, got back to our anchorage and found the *Thetis* at anchor having arrived from Chimbote.

13 November   Went round to Ancon for freight; received £55,000 in the evening; returned to our old anchorage. Heard the 1st Division of the Chilean Army had landed at Pisco.[118]

20 November   Dressed ship and saluted at noon in honour of the birthday of the Queen of Italy.[119]

21 November   Arrived HMS *Triumph* after an absence of nearly ten months.

23 November The *Christoforo Colombo*[120] arrived flying the broad pendant of Commander Lebrano[121]. Her speed is supposed to be about 17 knots but, as she is built of wood with only iron knees, she is unable to keep it up for any lengthened period for

---

117   A Lt Pedro Garezon used to be on the *Huascar.*
118   Coastal city, 145 miles south of Lima. Famous for its grapes, alcohol/eau de vie used to make Pisco Sour. Population: 4,000 (1876), 28,500 (1977), 82,000 (2005). Devastated by earthquakes, August 2007.
119   Princess Margherita of Savoy (1851-1926) = 1868 Umberto (1844-1900) who became King Umberto I 1878-1900. Rudolph had seen her from a distance in Rome, Whitsunday 1879.
120   Italian Flagship, built 1875.
121   Comandante Federico Labrano (1834-1896), later Admiral. (see photograph page 72)

fear of straining her. Her guns are light, six in number, she is with vertical cylinders and ten boilers, the upper part of her engines and boilers above the water line; she is nicely fitted up, the officers having very good quarters and she has always the advantage of being able to run away if necessary.

27 November   The Officers were very civil when we visited them. *Osprey* left for Pisco with Commander Acland[122] on board her having been selected to accompany the Chilean Army. All the neutral vessels sent a representative excepting the Germans.

1 December   *Thetis* arrived and left on the 2nd for Ancon.

6 December   *Osprey* returned 6th; on the morning of this day we had an entertainment in the way of the Chilean torpedo boats being fired upon by the batteries and the *Huascar* and *Pilcomayo* coming in to their assistance: the boats had followed a Peruvian launch filled with men and the latter made a lucky shot at the *Fresia* (the Thorneycroft) for she had to withdraw and sank off San Lorenzo in 7½ fathoms of water; the unfortunate engineer was closed up in his engine room and the door somehow was fastened from the outside and forgotten at the last moment; he was drowned.

7 December   The next day the Chileans set about raising her and succeeded when she was hauled up on shore for repairs. Every night *Pisagua*[123] was laying at anchor off Lorenzo and the work going on about the *Fresia*[124] but the Peruvians were too cowed to attempt to destroy both vessels. A good many shells from the batteries fell close to the ships and neutral hulks so we had all of us to shift another mile or so further down towards Ancon.

Exercised making runs with the Whitehead torpedoes.

---

122   Commander William Acland (1847-1924). Appointed 30 May 1874 HMS *Triumph* wrote: '*Six weeks with the Chilean Army – being a short account of a march from Pisco to Lurin and of the attack on Lima.*'
123   Chilean Ship.
124   Chilean Ship.

Map of the Lima Area.

8 December   Felt a heavy shock of an earthquake at 10.10 pm; it lasted about half a minute.

9/10 December   The *Angamos* came in within 8,000 yards and fired twelve shots into the town; on the latter day, she sent one shell right through the *Union* but fortunately for that ship it never burst. She was completely hidden by the sandbags breastwork erected for her protection so only the lower mastheads were visible. The *Angamos*'s fire was wonderfully true.

11 December   The next day she came in again to shell the *Union* but unfortunately the shot went in one direction and the gun, less the Trunnion coil which remained in the carriage, overboard; a Lieut. from the *Huascar* was killed as also No.1 of the Gun. Thus the famous *Angamos* gun came to an end, but there is no doubt that it did wonders and, but for the faulty construction of the gun, might have continued to do so. A pig boat (for so the *Angamos* was) became the scourge of the Peruvians and able to make beautiful firing at over 8,000 yards; she once fired at 11,000 or nearly that range. When she opened fire, two Peruvian launches filled with men and two small guns each came boldly to engage the *Angamos* on the chance of sinking her; the *Atahualpa* also got under weigh and steamed towards the blockaders in vain trying to entice them within range of the batteries but in vain.

The *Huascar*, *Chacabuco* and *Pilcomayo* took up the firing but were unable to hit either the *Urcos* or *Arno*[125]. Several of the shells burst close to the ships so most of them shifted berth again next day nearly another mile. We did not shift until the 13th when we drifted down under sail.

22 December   Went round to Ancon for refugees as the whole Chilean army were reported at Chilca within thirty-five miles of Lima. They were reported 26,000 strong of which 3,000 were cavalry, 2,000 artillery, rest infantry; they had 100 guns Krupp and Gatling. The 1st Division had marched from Pisco, the 2nd and 3rd landed at Chilca,

---

125   *Urcos* and *Arno*, Peruvian.

Canete[126], Cerro Azul[127] and other small bays in the vicinity; the Cavalry joining them from Pisco. On the way down we observed the *Loa* to be in Lat. 11˚57' 30" S, Long. 77˚13' W with her masts about twenty feet above the water and upright. We had a very bad 'painter' upon our arrival but it disappeared with the heavy shock of an earthquake. Found *Thetis* here, sent her on to Chimbote with mails. Embarked more freight computed amount on board £150,000.

25 December   Xmas day passed off quietly.

26 December   Several Men of War from Callao arrived going backwards and forwards with people for the hulks etc.

27 December   Embarked 260 men, women and children from the hulks where we arrived after dark; had rather an awkward business with the luggage and it got rather mixed, however we got all the people to their proper hulks. We found the *Gannet* had arrived.

(*28 December*[128])

30 December   *Osprey* sailed 'homeward bound'; we cheered her as she steamed round us. In the evening we had a dance which proved a success. Weather since the middle of the month exceedingly hot and stuffy, more particularly on shore.

---

126   Town 92 miles south of Lima.
127   Small town next to Canete.
128   28 December. The British cemetery near Callao records the burial on this day of Michael Gould of HMS *Shannon*. The cemetery records also list the following burials: Galsden, *Triumph*, 27 Dec 1879, Gilbert, *Triumph*, 16 Jan 1880, Ward, *Triumph*, 25 Jan 1880, Radford, Paymaster, 26 Jan 1880.

Granaderos a Caballo, 1881.

1881

ll communication cut off with Callao on 1 January 1881; so numbers of the hulks were towed round to Ancon whilst others remained as the English and French flagships intended to remain.

3 January 1881   Thick fog only lasted an hour or so.

6 January 1881   *Dayot*[1], French gun boat arrived, an exceedingly ugly old fashioned vessel.

10 January 1881   We went round to Ancon for refugees; the Chilean advance upon Lima being daily expected as they were known to (be) as far as Lurin[2] with their outposts towards Manchay and Chorillos. Heavy firing was heard from Lima and a good number of wounded were brought in; still Lima was filled with a crowd of officers in their glittering uniforms. Tonight I hear mentioned Lieut Carey Brenton[3] of the *Triumph* was specially selected as Attaché to the Peruvian army and his headquarters was mostly at the Hotel France & l'Angleterre.

12 January 1881   Wm Mills PRML[4] departed this life and was buried ashore the following day; he was a fine soldierly man very much liked by everyone and the finest looking man in the corps on board; poor fellow he was only twenty-five when he was cut off.

---

1   French Corvette, built 1869.
2   City, twenty-two miles south of Lima.
3   Lt Reginald O B Carey Brenton appointed 1 May 1878, HMS *Triumph*.
4   Private Royal Marine Light Infantry (PRML).

View of the Peruvian first line of defence with the burying party out after the assault. The extreme right shows the heights of Chorillos in rear as seen from the Villa and Lurin road.

The heights were stormed by the Atacama Regiment who lost 28 officers out of 35 and more than half their men.

General view of the battlefield taken from the left Peruvian Redoubt and looking down upon the plain, protected by a trench extending across it (about a mile in width).

General view of the battlefield at San Juan from the redoubt overlooking the farm of San Juan.

The first line of defence, view of redoubts and heights taken from near centre of position.

13 January 1881   This day an eventful one, for the long expected battle[5] took place, the Chileans had concentrated at Lurin and marched for the lines of San Juan[6]: the 1st and 2nd Division; the attack; the 3rd; the Reserve. The 1st Division on the left was told to attack the Redoubts in front of the Morro Solar[7] from the Villa[8] side and then the Morro Solar and Chorillos. The Chileans numbered 24,000; the Peruvians numbered about 30,000 men all told of which 8,000 (Reserve) were in the Redoubts[9] in the inner line of fortification at Miraflores. A perfect plain facing Lurin with a ridge of sand hills running across it at right angles varying from 3,000 to 6,000 feet in height crowned with lines of trenches defended on the flanks by small guns, about eighty in all. The Chilean attack was favoured by a slight fog, but as usual the Peruvians were quite content with their positions and had no outposts out. The Chileans slept during the night within 2,000 yards of the Peruvian lines without their having any knowledge of the fact. As dawn broke, the attack was made; the hardest fighting being on the Chilean left, the centre at San Juan was taken by the Esmeralda[10] and Buin[11] Regiments; the latter had to take a wide trench lined with Peruvians about ¹/₂ mile long[12] connecting two sand hills, crowned with sandbag batteries. The Buin advanced in skirmishing order, losing heavily until within about 300 yards when the defenders most them bolted; those who remained were shot or bayoneted. In less than two hours the heights of San Juan were taken when the cavalry attacked on the right a body of troops inside an enclosure, and here Colonel Yavar[13] of the Granaderos a Caballo[14], was shot; he was an old friend of ours and an exceedingly nice fellow. RIP.

Once inside, the Granaderos determined to revenge their Colonel's death and salved (i.e. slayed) something like 400 men who were too cowed to resist. The Atacama and

---

5   Markham tells us that the *Toro* bombarded Miraflores 15 Jan 1881.
6   Area south-east of Lima.
7   Impressive hill near Villa and Chorillos about 800 feet high and two miles in length.
8   Coastal area south of Lima; at that time an estate (hacienda) watered by a lake.
9   Some of these Redoubts have now been turned into landscaped memorial gardens.
10   Esmeralda Regiment, Chilean Manuel Abarca (see watercolour page 171).
11   Buin Regiment, Chilean.
12   First line of defence. (see several watercolours).
13   Coronel Tomas Yavar (?-1881). Chilean (see watercolour page 149).
14   Chilean Mounted Grenadier.

Unsuccessful attack on a redoubt near San Juan. Men could not be withdrawn and were all shot down, the wounded killed where they lay.

Coquimbo Regiments[15] attacked the Morro being assisted by this time by the artillery who were shelling it from Surco[16]. The Chacabuco were freed to retreat but, being reinforced by the Chiclano Regiment[17], stormed the Redoubt at the point of the bayonet. The Atacamas lost nearly half their men, the Coquimbo over forty per cent; the force 22 out of 35 officers; on their way up the Morro, so steep was it that the Atacamas had to lay

---

15   Coquimbo Regiment. Atacama Regiment: Chilean.
16   Village south of Lima.
17   Chacabuco Regiment, Chiclano Regiment; Chilean.

down for 20' (minutes) under fire to take breath before going on, and at one time were unable to make any headway; a Gatling in position had the exact range and swept them off as fast as they showed themselves over a ridge; a handful of men climbed upon the sea side of the Morro and got above the gun, fired upon the crew who bolted and gained the heights.

Everywhere boxes of ammunition strewn about many unopened, piles of dead horses and mules, the trenches lined inside with Peruvian dead, outside with Chileans who had gallantly rushed the Redoubts and fallen many of them against the very glacis of the works; when driven from the first line, many of the Peruvians retreated upon Chorillos where some hard street fighting took place which culminated in the utter

Sketch in a corner of a redoubt near the Villa Road.
An episode of the battle of Chorillos.

destruction of the place; the whole place was burnt, not a house left standing not even the English Minister's[18] and any people who were in Chorillos at the time were never seen again[19]. The officers were unable to restrain their men and perfect anarchy prevailed; finding no more Peruvians to kill, they formed two parties and began fighting amongst one another when a third party arrived to keep order; this was not

---

18   The English Minister's House: his summer residence.
19   Burning of Chorillos. Also described vividly by (Sir) Clements R Markham, *The War between Peru & Chile 1879-1882*, London 1883 p.252 and by Commander W Acland, *Six Weeks with the Chilean Army*, Norfolk Island, 1880 p.35.

done until over 200 had been killed! The scenes inside Chorillos are beyond description, the men rushing about maddened with fighting and liquor, burning and destroying the whole place. After the hard fighting, in which the Chilean army had taken positions which ought to have resisted the attack of more than double their numbers, they exposed themselves to utter destruction by their license and disorganisation in Chorillos. Commander Acland reports, 'If the Peruvians had attacked again that evening or night, the Chilean force might have been surprised and destroyed, but the truth was the Peruvians were anxious enough to retire to the lines of Miraflores and had had quite enough of it facing their adversary at San Juan'.

The HQs of the defence were at the latter place, but many of the officers thought Lima[20] a better place to be quartered, so used to spend the night in the capital and ride out after breakfast. Though there had been some heavy firing the previous evening, they did not break through their custom but remained as usual; when they did get out they found the positions had been taken in their absence. They had declared the Chileans would never attack in the early morning on account of the fog, but would remain in their

20   Lurin/Lima. Battlefield Plan, May 1881, black and white plan, page 154.

View of sand hills crowned with redoubts forming the 1st line of defence.

147

After the attack on San Juan, for nearly six miles of trenches, the slaughter was as shown.

Death of Colonel Yavar at the head of the Granaderos a Caballo at the Battle of Chorillos.

The Bay of Chorillos showing Barranco, with Andes beyond, 21 February 1881

The assault on No. 2 Redoubt at Miraflores, 2nd line of defence; redoubts protected by loop-holed 'adobe' walls lined with riflemen. The Chileans lost nearly 3,000 men, killed and wounded in this attack.

positions until it cleared otherwise they might lose their order or formation! Generally speaking it may be said that most Peruvians bolted when their enemy got within 3-400 yards. There were men struck down by Peabody Martin bullets at 2,500 yards but the Lima guns were not worth mentioning and were only effective up to 2,000 yards; still the battle was certainly an infantry one.

The cavalry, owing to the numerous dobie (adobe) walls being unable to be of much use and artillery firing at lines of trenches, did very little harm. As may be imagined, the panic in Lima at this time was considerable; the rifle firing being distinctly heard broken by the booming of the guns. The people began to realise it was nearing home and a rush was made to the Legations by the women and children. The English one had, at one time over 700, and the others, I believe, were pretty equally crammed. Every chair, every room, the balconies, crowded by anxious people in terror of being massacred by the Chileans.

The Ministers met and decided upon steps being taken to procure an armistice, so Brenton was sent off as Parliamentaire to the Chileans at Chorillos to find out if they were willing to treat and to prevent the destruction of Lima if possible.

13 January 1881   An Armistice was concluded until 12 pm 15 January; and the next morning all the authorities, Ministers, English and French Admirals went down to Miraflores to consult with Pierola as to the state of affairs; the latter seemed inclined to come to terms, for he saw the futility of continuing the struggle. They were at breakfast when suddenly heavy firing took place, bullets etc. flying all round them; there was immediately a rush, and away went Admirals, Ministers etc. at full speed[21] – the conference was at an end. It seemed as though the Chileans had broken faith and now wound up by attempting to murder the would-be peacemakers. They all arrived in Lima smothered in dust, but fortunately without damage, the French Admiral (du Petit-Thouars) was nearly cut down by a Peruvian dragoon, who was stationed with some men to kill anyone who attempted to run and mistook him for Montero. The US Minister Christiancy arrived exceedingly limp having run nearly all the way; coat torn, shirt unbuttoned. French Minister [was] very much washed out and fuming at the unseemly interruption. The German ditto nearly fainted and had to be assisted by the French Flag Lieut, who supported him in his arms; he arrived hardly recognisable, hat knocked in, livid and in a fainting condition; those who were present at the conference, state he was overcome 'even before the breakfast' (with what?). Mr St John[22] (Spenser)

---

21   Diplomats on the run. This incident is recorded by Acland p.37 and p.41 Markham p.254.
22   Mr Spenser St John FRGS FAS (1825-1910). Appointed to Lima 14 October 1874. British Embassy, Lima, records Spenser St John as being H.M. Consul General January 1878 – December 1881. Author of books on the Far East.

and the British Admiral arrived in the best condition of all; very dusty, coats flying away but still ready to run another mile if necessary; the latter was reported, to have been killed and G. Guly was sent down to Ancon on horseback to give the alarming news by which the late Senior on, the coast of Chile and Peru, was to become an Admiral after all and to take 'what steps he considered necessary in his new and exalted position'. The *Triumph* and *Victorieuse* in Callao Bay off the Rimac at once cleared for action and it seemed as though the *Shah* and *Huascar*[23] affair was again to be repeated but fortunately, a telegram arrived later on declaring all correct after all. The Peruvians in Lima fondly hoped the worst of the rumour for then they naturally thought the doom of Chile settled.

At the time of the Armistice, when it was granted, the Chileans were bringing up their guns and men to the furthest point occupied, and Baquedano accompanied by his staff, rode along the line to see everything necessary had been done to secure the positions they held; the men (Chileans) were at breakfast, not expecting any fighting at earliest before midnight the same day and were fraternising together, regiments mixed up with their arms piled and ammunition belts off.

Whether Baquedano actually overstepped the proper line of demarcation or not, will probably never be known, but it is certain, he and his staff were fired upon from a grove of trees by something like 150 riflemen and had a very narrow escape. The Chileans naturally thought they had been betrayed by Peruvian perfidy and the officer in charge of the batteries near Barranco[24] gave the order to fire which was done and returned by the Peruvians – Chileans without order rushed to the nearest stand of arms and cartridge belts and without being formed rushed on to the attack – the battle became general and an assault upon the celebrated Redoubts took place. On the left the Chileans were driven back, partly by the rifle fire from behind (adobe) dobie walls flanking the roads and in parallels perfect for the defence and loop holed, but not for long for they now formed and advanced; they themselves making use of the walls for

---

23   See *Naval Perspective* by Dr Celia Wu-Brading, page 18.
24   Barranco, a summer residential town a few miles south of Lima.

One of the guns destroyed by Chilean Cavalry with dynamite.

attack – a portion of the Reserves fought well and the Chileans lost heavily but nothing could resist the impetuousity of the attack.

Whole regiments of the defence cut and ran, rushing to the rear shouting 'Viva el Peru', the English Attaché expostulated with them and pointed out their enemy who was not in rear but in front of them – they ran the harder shouting more lustily than ever the same words; officers were seen smoking their cigarettes 300 or 400 yards from their men behind walls, their chief regret being, not that their men had run short of

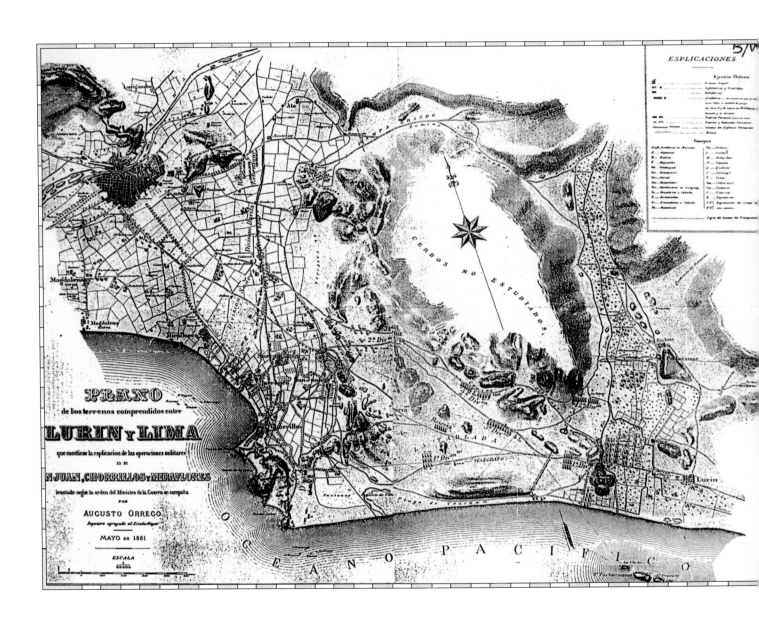

Lurin and Lima battlefield plan.

ammunition, but that their supply of matches was fast coming to an end. They never seemed to realise they were supposed to be fighting for their country; one really good Peruvian officer was killed *viz*; Colonel Castillo[25], first day's battle.

Barranco was partially destroyed as also part of Miraflores – most of the best houses; in front of a one gun battery and to the right of railway (looking east), land torpedoes were laid down (old Congreve rockets[26] closed with a detonator) and they blew up several of the cavalry who attacked and took the gun[27]. The moral effect of these torpedoes seems to have been great especially when the attack was made upon the Redoubts in front of San Juan; a good deal of hesitation was shown for a short time; the Chileans say they drove some 300 prisoners in front of them over the mined ground to blow up the mines. The cavalry attacking at the gallop suffered little on the whole from them, the torpedoes exploding as the horses' hoofs left the ground and merely lifted horse and rider into the air and numbers escaped with a severe shaking; in one place however twenty-five horses were killed and about half of their riders, but once inside, the troops who attacked over the mines, gave no quarter to the defenders within; in most cases, unless caught like a rat, they did not wait for quarter.

Our old friend L'Hermanda[28] came down on his head and was sent down to Chile quite mad; he was a very fine soldier and had been all his life engaged on the frontier of Araucania[29]. The Colonel of the Granaderos Yavar was killed at the head of his regiment in the 1st day's battle; his life was sacrificed by the Commander in Chief who ordered his regiment to attack a sand hill they could not ascend (west of San Juan). They however galloped round the front of it and charged inside an enclosure where some 400 odd Peruvians were concealed and, maddened by the loss of their Colonel, who was beloved and rightly too by all who knew him, they put them all to the sword; the Peruvians were regularly carved.

---

25 Coronel Fermin del Castillo (?-1881), Peruvian.
26 Invented by Sir William Congreve (1772-1828).
27 Incident probably illustrated by Rudolph's watercolour, page 153.
28 Chilean.
29 Old name for Chile.

Carson[30] and Urrutia[31] particularly distinguished themselves. The former had lost four brothers during the war. We knew the officers of this regiment very well having met them at Arica and ridden their horses frequently; our last salutation to them at Arica was 'hasta Lima'. Valdivieso, after the fall of Lima, became Commandante of the Palace and was as ready as ever to let us have horses.

The Chileans estimated the Peruvian losses in the two day's battle at 10,500 *viz*; 8,000 at San Juan or, as the Chileans call it Chorillos, and at Miraflores 2,500. Their own loss they estimated at over 5,000, but some of their officers who ought to know, say they lost nearly 6,000; when one considers the numbers engaged, the mortality was enormous; forty per cent of the Chilean officers engaged, were placed *hors de combat* whilst the Peruvians hardly lost any, and the day following the battle, Lima was crowded with officers in plain clothes. They had swaggered about the streets before the approach of the Chileans, smoking their cigarettes for the admiration of the fair sex and had impressed upon the latter that the Chileans, if they entered Lima, would commit every kind of excess, but the moment came, and they were not to the front to prevent them.

Canevaro (Peruvian Colonel)[32] seems to have behaved bravely; he was very badly wounded but recovered. After the second battle, the road to Lima from Miraflores was a wonderful sight; men, mules, carts etc. the former in many cases not having been near the scene of action, flying with the utmost rapidity for better quarters. Men and mules in numbers fell dead on the road and amongst the fields on the side of it, wounded no doubt at Miraflores. The greater part of the Peruvian troops quietly disbanded during the night and started off for their native mountains without food or anything; numbers would die on the way, but the Rabonas[33] led the way, prepared for hardships their husbands might be unable to endure.

15 January 1881   This night will long be remembered with shame by the Peruvians. Their own people attempted to burn Lima and then sack it and actually succeeded in

---

30 Chilean officer.
31 Chilean officer.
32 Coronel Cesar Canevaro (1846-1922), Peruvian.
33 Indian wives of Indian private soldiers acting as camp followers/cooks/nurses.

Destruction of the Union by Peruvians to prevent her falling into the hands of the Chileans.

The last of the Union; she sank in shoal water with her fore and main masts standing.

General view of Chorillos from the cliffs near Barranco
after the destruction of the place.

part, for at one time, Lima was burning[34] in three places; the whole of the Chinese quarter was destroyed and sacked, the unhappy Chinese murdered; and anyone who ventured into the streets was received with a shower of bullets.

The Chileans at any rate would only enter the ruins of Lima. It is only fair to say that these incendiaries were, though their numbers were considerable, of the lowest possible class and had a large proportion of niggers amongst them. The native women and the niggers produce a breed (for every kind of villainy) not to be equalled probably in any quarter of the globe, and once let these villains have the run of the streets and every kind of atrocity is committed.

Heavy firing in the streets continued all night and at 3 am the signalman on the top of the Legation informed me Callao was burning.

16 January 1881   We had a splendid view of the destruction of the Peruvian ships and Muelle Darsena[35], the *Union*[36] and *Limena*[37] steamed out clear of the docks and were then set on fire and left to their own devices. The *Union* sank near the beach with her upperworks out of water and fore and main masts standing; the others were 'burnt out' completely and continued drifting until stopped by the Chileans.

The vessels inside the docks burnt furiously, their masts going by the board and leaving nothing but the iron skin of the ships. The sparks, smoke etc. as their powder exploded, sent the debris up probably 200 feet or more. This took place as daybreak was dawning.

The Chileans sent in to Lima to say they would occupy the place in the morning and that, if a single man was fired upon in the streets, the city would answer for the consequences; as the place was in a state of anarchy, numbers of soldiers and citizens

---

34   Markham barely refers to this p.259 'Another tale of 2000 dead swelled the number of mourners in Lima. At 6.45 pm Miraflores was in flames. The savage victors sacked and burnt all the pleasant country houses, and destroyed the lovely gardens. This once charming retreat shared the fate of Chorillos and Barranco. It has become a wilderness of ruin and desolation.' The foreign residents and troops formed Fire Brigades and some are still called *Francia, Garibaldi*. Rudolph was made 'Honorary Fireman of Lima.' The other fire brigade was called *Bretagna*.
35   Callao docks and port.
36   Peruvian corvette built . . . . 1150 tons. Scuttled Callao 16 Jan 1881. See watercolours page 157.
37   Peruvian Transport, 1160 tons. Scuttled Callao 16 Jan 1881.

rushing about the streets, fully armed and in many cases half drunk, it was necessary at all costs to disarm them. The Urban Guard was then organised by M de Champeaux[38] (late Capt French Imperial Navy), the men turned out well, proceeded to the Palace where they were told off and Martinis[39] given them; after some firing in which all told about 120 of the niggers were killed, tranquillity was restored – but the main difficulty still remained to be solved: the Commander of the barracks and forts inside Lima refused to evacuate unless to superior orders; Colonel Suarez[40] who had become Commandante of Lima after the flight of Pierola, was recognised as head of the Government by the Santa Catalina men. After messages backwards and forwards, in which I explained to him from Mr St John (Spenser) if he did not evacuate and should he fire upon the Chileans, that the place would be destroyed, then he gave the order to his men to fall in.

The other commanders, finding the Santa Catalina fort was about to be evacuated, marched their men out and parties of the Urban guard took possession, until the arrival of the Chileans when they were turned over. Santa Catalina was turned over to me and taken possession of by sixty men who were placed in two reliefs on S Entry in the different places, magazines, etc. The Peruvians fell in and were marched out into the country. Whole stands of arms, about 25 or 30 field pieces, a few heavy guns, accoutrements of every description, hundreds. . . .[41]

---

38 Capitaine de Champeaux.
39 Invented by Hungarian Swiss Frederic Martini (1832-1897): a breech-loading mechanism for rifle.
40 Colonel Belisario Suarez V. (1833-1910), Peruvian.
41 See Epilogue.

A fortnight after the
battle of Chorillos this
was the scene on the
top of the Morro,
Chorillos.

Farewell to Coquimbo, Chile, 26 March 1881.

Epilogue

The diary is incomplete as it lacks the contents of Volume 2 but, at the front of Volume 1, there is luckily a complete log, 27 December 1878 to 16 June 1881.

Volume 2 was found in one of the Estate Deed Boxes but, unfortunately the first eleven pages have been cut out in such a way that it gives the impression that they were not removed in order to preserve them but purely to make use of the blank pages in the remainder of the book (printed by Waterlow & Sons Ltd, London Account Book manufacturers to Her Majesty's Government). The two lines below are therefore probably page 23. One has to hope that the mutilator first copied the text and that this will be discovered one day!

'up country and the beasts were to be sold for a dollar a head, but no one found it worth their while ever for the value of their skins and bones.'

From the Log Book, by the end of January 1881

HMS *Shannon* is 'Steaming off Ferrol Bay', Chimbote (North Peru) and are back 'At single anchor off Callao' by 2nd Feb.

They leave *c*7th March and are 'At single anchor off Coquimbo' (Chile) by 16 March; they depart on 26 March (see picture on page 161). They proceed through Magellan Straits (see picture on page 47) and are, by 23 April 'At single anchor off Montevideo'. They reach Plymouth on 16 June 1881.

An outpost at Monte Rico Chico
watching the fighting; standing by to give intelligence.

1994 Leicester Graphic

Continuing his study of a prominent County family, local historian Bernard Elliott profiles the life of one of his seafaring members.

udolph de Lisle has important historical significance in that he was a Catholic naval officer at a time when few catholic officers were to be found in the English navy. Born in 1853, Rudolph was the eighth son and fourteenth child of Ambrose and Laura Phillipps de Lisle. From an early age he loved the sea and his great desire was to pursue a career in the navy. After a short stay at Oscott College, from September 1865 to July 1866, he next attended Dr. Burney's Naval Academy at Gosport as a preparation for admission into the training ship *Britannia*. On 9 April 1867 he sat the examination for the *Britannia* passing 6th out of sixty-five successful candidates amongst a complement of 105. So, on 2 May 1867, he joined the *Britannia* where he remained until 2 July 1868. Passing out, he joined the *Victory* at Portsmouth as a midshipman and then, on 2 September 1868, was transferred to HMS *Bristol* at Spithead in which vessel he visited Gibraltar, Malta, Syracuse, Algiers and Lisbon. At Lisbon he was transferred to HMS *Penelope*, which returned to England in May 1869.

In the following months, thanks to the personal intervention of his naval great uncle Henry March Phillipps, he joined HMS *Barrosa*, which was one of the six ships of the First Flying Squadron organised by the Admiralty with a view to visiting the distant possessions of the Empire. Aboard the *Barrosa*, on 19 June 1869 he sailed from Plymouth for Yokohama before, in November of that year, embarking for Australia on

HMS *Liverpool*. On Christmas Eve, the *Liverpool* left Melbourne for New Zealand and at Wellington Rudolph met his brother-in-law, Sir Frederick Weld, Prime Minister of New Zealand. From New Zealand, Rudolph sailed back to England again via HMS *Liverpool* and so spent Christmas 1870 at home at Garendon. In April 1871, Rudolph joined HMS *Himalayas* at Plymouth from where he sailed to Panama to join HMS *Chameleon*. Aboard the *Chameleon* he visited Valparaiso, Vancouver, Honolulu and the South Sea Islands and, in December 1873, was promoted to the rank of Sub-lieutenant. Returning to Panama in the Spring of 1874, by December of that year he had become a full lieutenant. In May 1875 the *Chameleon* returned to England and Rudolph spent a couple of months at home at Garendon prior to his entering the Royal Naval College at Greenwich to undertake a course on gunnery. After completing the course successfully, in May 1876 he joined HMS *Pallas* which visited Constantinople as part of the fleet to help the Turks against the Russians. In July 1877 HMS *Pallas* sailed back to England and so, once more, Rudolph spent the Christmas of that year at Garendon, this time looking after his father during terminal illness. Ambrose died in March 1878 and soon after, in the April, Rudolph was assigned to HMS *Prince Albert,* then stationed at Devonport. In January 1879 he joined HMS *Shannon* which sailed to the Mediterranean and in June, Rudolph visited Rome.

From Italy, the *Shannon* sailed for South America so as to intervene in the war between Chile and Peru which had started in February 1879. Both sides claimed the rich nitrate field lying over the north of Chile and the south of Peru. Eventually the Chileans won the war, several battles in which were sketched by Rudolph. The sketches are still in possession of Squire de Lisle at Quenby Hall. In June 1881 the *Shannon* returned to England and so once more Rudolph found himself without a ship.

In July 1882, however, Rudolph managed to be assigned to a second gunnery course at the Royal Naval College, Greenwich. This course Rudolph also completed successfully and in November 1882 he joined HMS *Excellent*. His stay on that ship was short, for on 24 January 1883, he was told to report to HMS *Alexandra*, which was the flagship of the Mediterranean fleet whose Commander-in-Chief was Queen Victoria's second son, Alfred Duke of Edinburgh.

At this time, the Madhists were active in Egypt, and so in February 1884 the

Alexandra sailed for Alexandria to take part in operations against them. In May 1884 the *Alexandra* returned to Malta and from there sailed to Port Said. During these months, the Madhists were besieging Gordon in Khartoum and then in August 1884, orders came for the fleet to commence the ascent of the Nile as a means of saving General Gordon.

Over the next few months, Rudolph sent letter after letter to his mother, and this correspondence shows how a most gallant army marched and fought its way up the uncharted Nile. On 15 August Rudolph was part of a naval force made for Cairo and next Aswan. Near to Aswan they saw the ruins of Luxor of which Rudolph made a sketch. Then they passed the Tombs of the Kings and the two colossal figures of Rameses II and finally they reached Aswan. From Aswan a train took them to Ghizeh, where they boarded a steamer for Wadi Halfa. Here they disembarked and boarded a further train to reach the naval brigade at Akbar. On 3 September they boarded another steamer, which took them to the second cataract. 'The whole of the expedition', wrote Rudolph, 'is full of dangers to life and limbs'. On 1 November, Rudolph recorded that he was off with Commander Hamill to Tangier cataract by camel. When they arrived at Tangier, they found that the Nile had gone down seven feet. From Tangier the brigade moved on to Sennel, where, with an altar in a tent open to the sky, Rudolph heard Mass at the camp of the Canadians. On 7 December, Rudolph again went to Mass and that day he wrote to his mother, 'If only the Government had been able to make up its mind sooner, what a lot of lives would have been saved'.

Along its 850 mile course between Wadi Halfa and Khartoum, the River Nile describes two large curves in an S-Shape. To cut across the second of these a picked force under Sir Herbert Stewart traversed 150 miles of the desert. Rudolph was in this force and, at Abu Klea, the Mahdists attacked the English troops. Unfortunately the Gatling-gun (an early machine gun that had been invented by R.J. Gatling in about 1861) and which protected Rudolph's contingent, jammed, leaving them at the mercy of the Mahdists, who killed Rudolph and his fellow soldiers.

Bernard Elliott
Leicester Graphic, 1994

Ibis shot at Sandy Point c27 September 1879, See page 45

the Bay was very gay with the number of boats lodent
about & prepared to beau her in. The Batteries saluted
as she arrived; and the people on large were disappointed with her thinking she was as least as large as
the "Cochrane". Great numbers of people came on board
is soon to get a good view & we improved the occasion
by having an impromptu dance. & did the error touch
a belief that numbers came off neat day to see the ship
We had dancing twice & found the Chilean ladies had
not deteriorated in appearance. I found several of
my old friends amongst the de Peralta's in great form and as
kind as ever and as hospitable, made several new acquaintance
at their house. Oct 21st Left Valparaiso for Coquimbo
Moderate Sw winds made all plain sail
22nd 7am Stopped Engines 23rd 11am Commenced steaming
8am Furled sails 11.45 am anchored in Coquimbo Bay
in 18 1/2 fms. Send 5 us Practiles. Found the Liffey
stns ship. U.S. Flagship Pensacola (R. Admiral Rodgers)
stayed here until the 28th when we were ordered off by
having Chilean Expeditionary force had sailed for the
coast of Peru & we had instructions to keep them in sight.
The sea breeze set in generally about 11. from the Sw & fails

Page 59/60 from diary, 21 Oct 1879.

Huacho and Arica. The two shipmates -
the Shannon's pets

Appendix 2

Report enclosed with letter dated 27 May 1879
from the Manager of the Tarapaca Nitrate Co., oficina
Limena, la Noria, Iquique, to Mr C.J. Hayne, partner of
William Gibbs & Co., Valparaiso

t 6.30 on the morning of the 21st, inst. two large vessels coming from the north were observed to be standing in for the harbour of Iquique.

They were at first supposed, by those on shore, to be the two Chilean iron-clads returning from their expedition to Arica, but little interest was taken in their movements. As they approached the land however, it was seen first that they were not the enemy's ships, and shortly after that they were the long hoped for Peruvian men of war the *Huascar* and the *Independencia*. The news flew round the town and all Iquique turned out to witness the expected combat. The excitement was intense; the beach, the roofs of houses, every point of vantage were thronged with people eagerly watching the manoeuvres of the ships in the bay and waiting almost with bated breath the issue of the fight.

The Chilean ships, of which there were three in the harbour, the *Esmeralda*, the *Covadonga* and a transport the *Lamar,* were evidently taken by surprise; their aimless movements across the bay and back again, the transport hauling up American colours and lowering them again showed they were at a loss how to act, meanwhile the *Huascar* and the *Independencia* steamed steadily on, gradually slowing down as they approached the land. At length, the Chileans seemed to come to a decision, the transport steered out at full speed for the south, driving and doing all she could to get away, while the *Esmeralda* and the *Covadonga* slowly moved into position for the engagement. At 7.45, the *Huascar* flung out the red and white colours of Peru, let fly a cannon shot that dropped just between the two Chilenos and then moved off as if intending to pursue the retreating transport. The *Covadonga* however, who was the first to reply, fired two or three well directed shots into the *Huascar*, which seemed to alter her intention and she directed her course once more towards the two remaining ships. To meet the difficulty of engaging the enemy without endangering the town by stray shots, the *Huascar* and *Independencia* worked round to the north leaving open the course to the south, the *Covadonga*, seeing a chance of escape immediately took advantage of it, slipped out, and ran for Chile. The *Independencia* instantly followed her, leaving the *Huascar* to try conclusions with the *Esmeralda* alone. Checking, the English pilot had boarded the *Huascar* previously when off the island, and during the movements that followed, he acted as pilot.

Owing to fear of torpedoes, the *Huascar* did not come into the harbour, she laid some distance off and kept up a hot fire upon the *Esmeralda,* who replied smartly and well. Finally, the *Huascar* worked round behind the island and fired across it, being assisted in her endeavours to dislodge the *Esmeralda* by several field pieces firing from the mainland. This artillery duel continued until about 11 am when the *Esmeralda*, finding her position untenable, moved away to the other side of the bay, the *Huascar* steamed across to her and the fight began in deadly ernest. The *Huascar* charged straight at her and rammed her hard, being met by a broadside from the *Esmeralda*'s heavy guns and a tremendous fusillade from marksmen in the rigging and other parts of the ship. The *Huascar* drew off, fired into the enemy, and rammed at her again being met as before by a well directed broadside, followed by a desperate attempt at boarding. The commander of the *Esmeralda*, Captain Prat, leapt on board the *Huascar*, revolver in hand, followed by a daring few, but they were shot down almost before they had time to strike a blow. Captain Prat got as far as the the turret, where he killed Lieutenant S. Velarde, but was himself shot a moment after by a seaman. By this time, it was apparent that the wooden sides of the *Esmeralda* had been crushed in by the ponderous ram of the *Huascar,* and that she was sinking fast, though her fire never slackened for an instant. A third time the *Huascar* charged her, and in two minutes down went the ship and her gallant crew, she sank colours high and when her bows were under water, she fired off her two stem guns as a parting defiance to her foe. The Chilean flag was the last that was seen of the *Esmeralda*. Out of a complement of 200 men, but 35 were saved, nearly all foreigners, a large proportion being Englishmen.

During the progress of the battle, the little *Covadonga* had been running south, followed closely by the *Independencia*. Shots were exchanged but the *Independencia*'s fell wide of the mark while, as well as could be seen, nearly every shot of the *Covadonga*'s told. After clearing the island, she (the *Covadonga*) seemed to be steering to Gruesa Point, but when off Cavancha she altered her course and kept close inshore, creeping slowly along, the *Independencia* some distance off but gradually drawing up. After clearing Gruesa Point, the *Covadonga* steered out west for some time then suddenly altered her course to the south. The *Independencia* thinking to cut her off steered straight in, holding to her course, and in a few minutes crashed with all her weight and the force of her powerful engines on to the rocks.

She, at once heeled over, one side nearly under the water, the other so high that her guns could not be used. The *Covadonga,* seeing that she had struck and was lying stranded and helpless, at once returned and blazed into her at very close quarters till, the *Huascar* looming up, warned her it was time to be off. And so by pluck, stratagem and knowledge of the coast, she escaped.

It was soon seen that it was hopeless attempting to do anything for the *Independencia*, the *Huascar* tried to tow her off, but she was hard and fast. The remainder of her crew were transferred and she was fired, and all that remains of the fine iron-clad, the *Independencia*, her guns and stores, is a black hulk stranded on the rocks outside Gruesa Point. Of the crew, two-thirds were shot or drowned, including Lieutenant D.G. Garcia y Garcia. And so ended this most disastrous victory.

Manuel Abarca,
Esmeralda Regiment, Chilean

Sketch showing
accoutrements.

Bibliography

Acland, Comdr W.RN (1847-1924), *Six Weeks with the Chilean Army*, Norfolk Island, Pacific, 1880

Alisky, M, *Historical Dictionary of Peru*, London, 1979

Barrios, D.W. & Antezana, J., *Diccionario Historico Geografico de Tacna*, 1974

Basadre, J., *Peruanos del Siglo XIX*, Lima, 1981

Bizzaro, S., *Historical Dictionary of Chile*, 1972

Boyd, R.B., *Sketches of War 1879-1880*, London, 1881

Buendia, Gen J. (1816-1895), *Guerra Con Chile,* Lima, 1967

Caceres, Mariscal AA (1833-1923), *Memorials de la Guerra Con Chile* (1924), Lima, 2 vols, 1979

Calvo y Perez, Dr M., *Resumen Historico del Peru*, Lima, 1940

Cespedes, Mario & Garreau, Lelia, *Gran Diccionario de Chile,* 2 vols, 2nd ed., 1986

(Diccionario), *Enciciopedico del Peru*, 5 vols, 1966

Doering, J.G., *Planos de Lima*, 1613-1983, Lima, 1983

Fuentes, Jordi, *Diccionario Politico de Chile*, 1967

Guerra Mariniere, Margarita, *La Guerra Con Chile*, Lima, 1996

Guerra Mariniere, Margarita, *La Occupacion de Lima*, Lima, 1991

Harriman, Brenda, *The British in Peru*, Peru, 1984

Higgins, J., *Lima*, Oxford, 2005

Lopez, J., *Historia de la Guerra del Guano – Salitre* (1930), Lima, 2 vols, 1979

Manning, Capt, T.D. & Walker, Comdr C.F., *British Warship Names*, London, 1959

Milla Batres, C., *Recopilacion de Partes & Documentos*, Lima, 2 vols, 1979

Markham, Sir C. (1830-1916), *The War Between Peru & Chile 1879-1882,* London, 1883

Mathew, W.M., *The House of Gibbs & the Guano Monopoly*, London, 1981

(Ministerio de Guerra), *La Gesta de Limas 1881-1891*, Lima, 1981

Naylor, B., *Accounts of the 19th Century, South America*, London, 1969

Neuhaus, R.P.C., Navegando Entre El Peru y Ancon, 1998 – Damas, Poder y Politica en el Peru, 2007

Oxenham, Rev. H.N. (1829-1888), *Memoir of Lt Rudolph de Lisle RN*, London, 3rd ed., 1887

Paz Soldan, M.F. (1821-1886), *Narracion Historica de la Guerra* (1887), Lima, 3 vols, 1979

Revue Maritime & Coloniale, *V. Admiral Bergase du Petit Thouars*, (1832-1890), Paris, 1890

Robinson, A.R.B., *The Magnificient Field of Enterprise: Britons in Peru 1815-1915*, Lima, 1997

Sater, W.F., *Chile & The War of the Pacific*, 1986

Shakespeare, N., *The Vision of Elena Silves*, (1989), London, 2004

Stewart, W., Henry Meiggs (1811-1877), *Yankee Pizzaro*, USA, 1946

Vargas, U. Rev. R. (1886-1975), *Historia General del Peru,* Vols. IX, X, Barcelona, 1971

Vargas, U. Rev. R., *Guerra Con Chile 1879-1883*, 2 vols, Lima, 1967/1970

Vargas, U. Rev. R., *Historia General de la Guerra del Pacifico,* Lima, 2 vols, 1970

Wu-Brading, Dr Celia, *Testimonios Britanicos*, Lima, 1986

Rudolph de Lisle RN

Leicester, 1867
(Burton)

Sudan, 1885

1861 (Lou Fisher of Grantham)

Lima 1880 (Courret Hermanos)

London, C1881 (Elliott and Fry)

Index